# TOM PAINE

*Books by the Same Author*

DOCTOR DARWIN (Erasmus Darwin)

THE SMITH OF SMITHS (Sydney Smith)

THE FOOL OF LOVE (William Hazlitt)

THOMAS PAINE
After the portrait by Romney

# TOM PAINE

# PAINE

## *Friend of Mankind*

---

*By* HESKETH PEARSON

---

*PUBLISHERS*

HARPER & BROTHERS

*New York and London*

MCMXXXVII

TO

MALCOLM MUGGERIDGE

# CONTENTS

# ILLUSTRATIONS

## *AUTHOR'S NOTE*

FOR facts and information about Thomas Paine no one at this date can add much to Moncure Conway's exhaustive (and exhausting) biography. But in art the daub of hagiography is no less a blemish than the smudge of iconoclasm, and his desire to enshrine Thomas as a secular saint prevented Conway from portraying Paine as a credible human being.

I have consulted all the original sources, Chalmers, Cheetham, Cobbett, Sherwin, Rickman, Yorke, Morris, Vale, etc., and have written of Paine primarily as a man, not as the founder of a faith or the formulator of a political philosophy. Creeds die; humanity endures; and human beings are much more interesting than their causes or their beliefs.

# TOM PAINE

"A statue of gold ought to be erected
to you in every city in the universe."
*(Napoleon I to Thomas Paine.)*

"His writings certainly had a powerful
effect on the public mind."
*(George Washington.)*

# Chapter I

## FIRST TROUBLES

43294

ALTHOUGH attempts have been made to prove that the parents of Thomas Paine were descended from highly respectable Norfolk families, because most biographers like their subjects to be well-born, the known facts are that Joseph Paine was a Quaker and stay-maker, and that Frances Cocke was the daughter of an attorney and a member of the Church of England. Frances was eleven years older than Joseph, and this, together with their poverty and dissimilar religious tastes, may have helped to make her ill at ease. She was described as "a woman of sour temper and an eccentric character," while her husband had the reputation of being "though poor, an honest man."

Their son Thomas was born at Thetford, Norfolk, on the 29th of January, 1737, and was educated at the local grammar school. He did not learn Latin, partly because he did not wish to and partly because the

Quakers, to which body he officially belonged, did not approve of the Latin authors; but he had sufficient curiosity to discover what the classics were about. For moral instruction his father took him in hand, with permanent effect on his character. "The natural bent of my mind was to science," he wrote in after life. "I had some turn, and I believe some talent, for poetry; but this I rather repressed than encouraged, as leading too much into the field of imagination." Such samples of his verse as have come down to us suggest that "aptitude" would have described his turn for poetry better than "talent," but the interesting point in this confession lies in the Quakerish determination to check a natural instinct. Later he was to perceive the flaws in his upbringing: "Though I reverence their philanthropy, I cannot help smiling at the conceit, that if the taste of a Quaker could have been consulted at the creation, what a silent and drab-colored creation it would have been! Not a flower would have blossomed its gayeties, nor a bird been permitted to sing."

There must have been a fight for the soul of Tom in the family circle, because his maternal aunt managed to get him confirmed in the parish church at Thetford and sometimes read sermons to him in which the beliefs of the orthodox religion were set forth in somber terms. "I well remember, when about seven or eight years of age, hearing a sermon read by a relation of mine, who was a great devotee of the church, upon the subject of what is called *Redemption by the death of the Son of God*. After the sermon was ended, I went into the garden, and as I was going down the garden steps (for I perfectly recollect the spot) I revolted at the recollection of what I had heard, and thought to myself that it was making God Almighty act like a passionate man, that killed his son, when he could not revenge himself any other way; and as I was sure a man would be hanged that did such a thing, I could not see for what purpose they preached such sermons. This was not one of those kinds of thoughts that had anything in it of childish levity; it was to me a serious reflection, arising from the idea I had that God was too good to do such an action, and also too almighty to be under any necessity of doing it. I believe . . . that any system of religion that has anything in it that shocks the mind of a child, cannot be a true system."

His parents "distressed themselves," as he put it, in order to keep him at the grammar school, and he appraised the value of his training with exactitude: "As to the learning that any person gains from school education, it serves only, like a small capital, to put him in the way of beginning learning for himself afterwards. Every person of learning is finally his own teacher." At the age of thirteen he left school and for about four years he worked in his father's business, making stays and fitting bodices for the ladies of Thetford. This occupation did not appeal to a youngster who was one day to become famous for re-making states and formulating policies; and, in a fit of romantic ardor, inflamed by the picturesque imagination of a schoolmaster who had once served on a man-of-war, he made an attempt to join the crew of a privateer, the *Terrible*, whose captain owned to the rather forbidding name of Death. Paine senior heard of the boy's intention in time, followed him on board, and administered a strong dose of Quaker doctrine. Tom was suitably impressed and returned for a while to stay-making, but the effect of his father's admonitions was not lasting and he went to sea in another privateer, the *King of Prussia*. Quickly convinced that life on the ocean was only picturesque when viewed from the shore, he left his ship at the earliest opportunity and went to London, where he found work with a stay-maker in Hanover Street, Long Acre, studying philosophy and astronomy in his spare time.

In 1758 he moved to Dover. He was now twenty-one, an age when most ambitious young men became impatient and begin to wonder whether they are making the most of their opportunities, whether they have chosen the right profession, and whether they ought not to be independent of others. Paine felt no secret urge to go on making stays for the rest of his life, yet he could see no better living in any other profession, so he determined to start work on his own account. By establishing friendly relations with the daughter of his employer he managed to borrow some money from the latter, and with this he set up as a master stay-maker at Sandwich, where he lodged in the market-place. His business did not prosper and his position was not improved by marriage with a pretty waiting-maid, Mary Lambert, and residing on Dolphin Key. He left Sandwich within a year to make a fresh start at Margate, where his wife died in childbirth and where he soon abandoned the trade of stay-making.

Still anxious to increase his knowledge, he went to London and would no doubt have remained there if lack of money had not forced him to adopt a profession in which he could earn some. He discovered that the job of an exciseman was comparatively easy and would give him a number of hours for leisure and meditation. Returning home to Thetford, he divided his time between philosophy and the excise, being appointed as a gauger at Grantham towards the end of 1762. Two years later he was at Alford, risking his life for a salary of £50 a year. His job was to catch smugglers, who when caught were expert in the use of the knife, and to make himself disliked by the traders of excisable commodities. In those days the most unpopular person throughout the countryside was the exciseman. The rich objected to him because he increased the cost of their luxuries, the poor hated him because he stood in the way of their necessities, and both classes sided with smugglers and traders against the officious government man. Paine's sympathies were with the poor, and as he happened to be one of them himself he was careful to minimize the risks of his profession. The smugglers of Alford came and went on their unlawful occasions and the books of the traders in the district were not subjected to personal scrutiny. The unexpected arrival of a supervisor, who discovered that Paine had passed the traders' returns without examining their stocks, resulted in his dismissal from the service in August, 1765.

Again he made stays, this time at Diss in Norfolk, but the business had now become so distasteful to him that he quarreled with everybody and at the age of twenty-eight became a schoolmaster, first in Goodman's Fields, London, where he taught English on a salary of £25 a year, and then at a school in Kensington. He probably taught himself more than his pupils, for he once confessed that as a schoolmaster he had "derived considerable information; indeed I have seldom passed five minutes of my life, however circumstanced, in which I did not acquire some knowledge." But he was still seriously concerned about his future and even attempted to take orders in the Church of England, which would have left him time to study philosophy. The attempt failed and he applied for restoration to the excise. Since his misdemeanor had been a common one, most excisemen preferring a quiet life to a cut throat, he was reinstated, and in February, 1768, he became the excise officer at Lewes, Sussex.

He lodged at Bull House with a Quaker tobacconist

named Samuel Ollive. Although he had always regarded the business of politics as contemptible, for "it presented to my mind no other idea than is contained in the word jockeyship," he strongly inclined towards the principles of the Whigs and joined a social club which met in the evenings at the White Hart Tavern. In this circle he soon became notable for the vigor of his debating powers, the independence of his opinions and the obstinacy with which he supported them. The club was a convivial one and the arguments were often both long and warm, Paine invariably having the last word, for he could outargue any of his opponents and talk them under the table. He wrote humorous poems, a few serious ones, and a number of papers on such subjects as the absurdity of dueling, international arbitration, justice for women, mercy for animals, and the crime of slavery. His duties took him to Brighton (then known as Brighthelmstone) and other places, his reputation as an outspoken and dogmatic champion of unpopular causes spreading wherever he went. He was liked as much as an exciseman could be liked because he shut an eye to the delinquencies of poor tradesmen and was not above standing a superior in the service one or two bottles of wine to make him equally blind. Questioning nothing, severe to no one, he was a bad exciseman, a benevolent man.

Samuel Ollive died in the middle of 1769 and for a while Paine lodged elsewhere, but wishing to increase his meager salary he went into partnership with Ollive's widow and daughter in 1770, opening a shop and selling groceries as well as tobacco. The daughter, Elizabeth Ollive, was a girl of twenty and pretty enough to "attract men of higher rank and greater delicacy" than Paine, as his earliest biographer phrases it. But with her Quaker upbringing it is not surprising that she preferred an intelligent human being to brainless fox-hunters or elegant nonentities, and in March, 1771, she became Mrs. Thomas Paine.

The marriage was not a success, though none of Paine's biographers has been able to provide a reasonable explanation. The facts can be stated briefly. There was no sexual relationship between them during the three and a quarter years of their married life; they occupied different beds; and when Mrs. Paine complained to friends that their marriage had never been consummated, so much local scandal was created that Paine was taxed on the subject. He flatly refused to discuss the matter: "It is nobody's business but my own," he said. "I had cause for it, but I will name it to no one." This did not satisfy the scandal-mongers, who went about saying that he was the victim of "natural imbecility" or of "philosophical indifference." Hoping, no doubt, that a straightforward business statement would appeal to his critics, Paine made it known that he had "married for prudential reasons and abstained for prudential reasons," and after the two had agreed to separate he declared that he no longer found a wife a convenience. The scandal increased in volume and at last he was openly charged with a want of virility. This touched his pride and he actually agreed to be medically examined. One doctor reported that he saw "apparent ability," another that there was "no natural defect." Armed with these testimonials to his manhood, Paine arranged a legal separation from his wife in June, 1774, in which he gave up all his rights in her property. Thereafter he always spoke of her with tenderness and sometimes sent her pecuniary aid without telling her from whom it came.

Strange though it must appear to those who are so busy looking for obscure motives that they cannot perceive plain facts, Paine's simple explanation of his conduct is the correct one, though it requires amplification. He married for prudential reasons: that is to say, he wanted a home in which he could be comfortable and a business on which he could live, since the salary of an exciseman, after necessary expenses had been deducted, was little more than £30 a year. He abstained for prudential reasons: that is to say, he could not afford the luxury of children. It is almost certain that he was not in love with his wife, and, not being a sensualist, he did not desire what he could not love. Like all people who think for themselves, he had a moral code of his own, and while he thought there was no harm in providing himself with a home at a woman's expense, he would not go farther and enslave her to a family which he might not be able to support. Also, being of an intensely humane disposition, the death of his first wife in childbirth may have influenced him to avoid the risk of a similar catastrophe.

From the woman's point of view, since she was fond of him, he was of course a callous husband. From his point of view, since he was not fond of her, he was a considerate one. His mother agreed with his wife, for when she received news of their separation she wrote a letter of sympathy to Elizabeth, in which she declared that Tom had been an undutiful son (apparently because he had not written to her for two years, nor had he repaid a loan of £20) and it naturally followed that he was "the worst of husbands."

The fact is that Paine was not a domestic man. Like another famous reformer, he would have denied his family in the interests of humanity. He needed disciples, not relations. Already, at Lewes, while neglecting his wife he was serving a cause. His fellow-excisemen were agitating for higher wages; they wished to bring their grievances before Parliament; and they chose Paine to act as their representative. He wrote an appeal for them, distributed it in the proper quarters, went to London to canvass the politicians, got into touch with Oliver Goldsmith and others whose aid might be useful, and exerted himself in every possible way to bring about the desired effect. Needless to say his labors were wasted.

The excisemen were unpopular everywhere; no public support for their plea was forthcoming; and the politicians were not likely to put themselves out for a poverty-stricken section of the community which annoyed everybody who had the power to put them in. Incidentally Pitt and Dundas, like many politicians before and after them, made the most of both worlds. They received large consignments of smuggled goods and enforced the taxes with vigor; in their public characters they aided the excisemen, in their private characters they abetted the smugglers. Paine had not learned the proper method of approaching politicians; and as their incomes would have been unaffected by an increase in the salaries of state servants, their feelings remained unaffected.

By his efforts in this cause Paine became a marked man. Governments have a habit of regarding anyone who wants butter on his bread as a political agitator. Very soon he will be asking for jam on his butter, and even—who knows?—for meat with his tea. Revolutionary propaganda of this kind has to be checked. It was impracticable to discharge all the signatories to the appeal, because without the excise there could be no sinecures, but a scapegoat had to be found; and who better than the writer, the leader of the revolt? It was easy to discover a pretext: Paine had been absent from business without leave. As a matter of fact, he had spent so much time over the appeal that his business had been neglected, debts had accumulated, and when it became

known that his attempts to get better pay for excisemen
had failed his creditors pounced. Being in danger of
arrest, he hid from the law officers in the cock-loft of
the White Hart Tavern, where he remained until Sun-
day set him free, when he left Lewes. The authorities
acted with a promptness only displayed by public bodies
when it serves their purpose, and Thomas Paine was
discharged for the second time from the excise, on April
8, 1774.

His household furniture and business stock were sold
to pay his creditors, and having settled his domestic
affairs with a legal separation from his wife he left for
London in the following June. He was now thirty-seven
years old, without a profession, with no chance of earning money, and with a strong taste for philosophy and
science. He lived in a garret in Ailiffe Street, an obscure part of the City, and for a few months existed as
a hack writer. He met Benjamin Franklin, who taught
him a lot about electricity and thought him "an ingen-
ious worthy young man." As a child he had read a natural history of Virginia, which had made him anxious to
visit America, and now Franklin advised him to try his
luck on the other side of the Atlantic. Already he was
beginning to take an interest in politics and Franklin
doubtless felt that America was a safer place for Paine's
peculiar views than England, for though the Colonists
were still loyal to the crown, they would not be likely

to lock him up for saying that a monarchy was "debasing to the dignity of man."

Paine's attention had been turned towards statecraft by the casual remark of a tradesman. "After playing bowls at Lewes," he once told a friend, "retiring to drink some punch, Mr. Verral, one of the bowlers, observed, alluding to the wars of Frederick, that the King of Prussia was the best fellow in the world for a king—he had so much of the devil in him. This, striking me with great force, occasioned the reflection that if it were necessary for a king to have so much of the devil in him, kings might very beneficially be dispensed with.

The man who had failed as a stay-maker, a sailor, a schoolmaster, and an excise officer, left London in October, 1774, and landed in America on November 30th. It is possible that, if the authorities in England had been able to foresee the result of his departure, they would have given him another chance in the excise.

## Chapter II

### UNITING THE STATES

THERE was a pleasing simplicity about Thomas Paine. The majority of people who start life with ideals for the betterment of mankind shed them by degrees from the age of twenty onwards, and by the time they reach forty they are fairly well hardened into a conviction that mankind cannot be bettered, whether regarded as a joke or a failure. But after a number of experiences that would have turned anyone else into a cynic or a criminal, Paine commenced a life of selfless devotion to the cause of humanity at an age when most human beings are solely concerned with their financial stability and personal comfort.

His domestic life had given him nothing; it would have been better for him (and his wives) if he had never married. His trade of stay-making had brought him little but starvation and irritation. His job as an exciseman had been taken from him, in the first case because he was too indulgent to individuals, in the second because he had fought for his fellows. He had experienced the impotence of poverty and witnessed the indifference of the powerful. He had been familiar from childhood with the un-Christian rivalry of sects; he had learned the uselessness of attempting to argue men out of their prejudices; and he had come to the unavoidable conclusion that the mass of mankind were more interested in wars, quarrels, jealousies, sports, and other forms of silly rivalry, than in bettering their condition or improving their minds by the study of philosophy and science.

Yet, in spite of all he had known and all he had read, he faced life at the age of thirty-eight as a complete and unrepentant idealist. He believed in the essential nobility of man. He believed that if people were free they would be good: economic freedom would naturally follow political freedom; social freedom would inevitably result from religious freedom; wars would cease when monarchs were deposed; happiness would ensue when men directed their own destinies; under a truly representative and democratic government, solely concerned with law and order, mankind, not its masters, would inherit the earth, which would then resemble the Kingdom of Heaven.

The Paine program was simple, if comprehensive, and sound enough to have worked admirably if only men and women had been what Paine then thought they were. But as they remain what he discovered them to be after sacrificing himself in the interests of humanity for twenty-odd years, the Kingdom of Heaven has not yet appeared on the map of the world.

Paine took with him to America a letter of introduction from Franklin to his son-in-law, in which it was suggested that Tom might be useful as a clerk, an assistant tutor, or an assistant surveyor. As a result he managed to get a certain amount of tutoring and before long he was helping a printer and bookseller to run a new publication called the *Pennsylvania Magazine*. Soon he was appointed editor at £50 a year and the papers he had written at Lewes began to make their appearance. Religion and politics were forbidden themes, and the magazine was largely devoted to descriptions of such useful, if unexciting, objects as threshing- and spinning-machines, but Paine quickly increased the circulation with articles on more human and debatable topics. Anticipating by a month the formation of the first American Anti-Slavery Society, he courageously advocated freedom for Negroes nearly a century before they got it; he urged the abolition of war as a means of settling international disputes; he described monarchy and hereditary titles as anachronisms; he denounced cruelty to animals, exposed the crime of poverty in states calling themselves civilized, argued in favor of international copyright laws, and in fact provided powder and shot for all the world-reformers and all the progressive parties of the following century. Within the anthropoid limitations of human nature there are still possibilities of improvement along the lines he laid down.

Among the many rational views that appeared under many pseudonyms (for he wrote nearly the whole paper) he advanced the opinion that women should not be enslaved "by indissoluble ties" to the rude and the brutal, and from his own experience drew this picture of married life: "As ecstasy abates coolness succeeds, which often makes way for indifference, and that for neglect. Sure of each other by the nuptial bond, they no longer take any pains to be mutually agreeable. Careless if they displease, and yet angry if reproached; with so little relish for each other's company that anybody else's is more welcome. . . ." He was probably the first person to display an entirely civilized attitude towards women, and the movement for female emancipation may be said to have begun with his words: "When they are not beloved they are nothing; and when they are they are tormented. They have almost equal cause to be afraid of indifference and love. Over three-quarters of the globe Nature has placed them between contempt and misery."

Before Paine had been five months in America something occurred which concentrated all his thoughts and energies on one subject. For many years the American Colonies had been bullied by the home government and

a crisis was reached when it was proposed to garrison a
standing army in the Colonies and enforce a stamp tax
to keep it there. Speeches were made, resolutions were
carried, protests were registered, petitions were sent off,
riots occurred, and the Stamp Act was repealed in 1766.
All the same the English Parliament maintained its
right to tax the Colonies without reference to the people
taxed, and a year later an import duty was placed on tea
and other commodities, the revenue so obtained to be
used for the salaries of Crown officials in the Colonies.

The Americans declined to buy English tea and in
Boston they tumbled it into the sea. George III lost his
temper; he ordered Parliament to remove the capital
of Massachusetts from Boston to Salem, to annul the
Colony's charter, and to arrange for the transportation
and trial of those citizens who had proved their disloyalty to the Crown by refusing to drink English tea. The
other Colonies rallied to the support of Massachusetts
and a Continental Congress at Philadelphia drafted an
appeal to the king and people of England and Canada,
in which the notion of independence was scouted but the
right to tax themselves was claimed. George III, however, was not to be cheated of his prey; an army was sent
out under General Gage, who was appointed military
and civil governor of Massachusetts; and the Americans
began to prepare for trouble. One of Gage's first jobs
was to arrest Samuel Adams, who had organized the
"Boston tea-party," and John Hancock, another strong

patriot. They were in hiding at Lexington, but left hurriedly the moment warning came that troops were on the way to capture them. A body of armed Americans, ready on the spot to act in an emergency, had been told not to fire unless the British troops fired at them first. An unknown soldier in the American ranks got excited, pulled his trigger, and though the gun missed fire the flash was seen and the British replied with a volley. Seven patriots lay dead on the ground, "the massacre at Lexington" passed into history, and Thomas Paine wrote to Benjamin Franklin: "I thought it very hard to have the country set on fire about my ears almost the moment I got into it."

The Lexington affair occurred on April 19, 1775, and from that moment Great Britain was at war with her American colonies. There was another Congress at Philadelphia and George Washington was appointed commander-in-chief of the American forces. More soldiers were rushed from England. Howe, Clinton, and Burgoyne arrived at Boston with an additional ten thousand men. The battle of Bunker Hill was fought on June 17th. Yet in spite of the defeat sustained by the Americans and the obvious intention of the home government to crush all resistance and to impose the will of a rather foolish Hanoverian gentleman on a continent he knew nothing about, there was scarcely a murmur of disloyalty on the part of the leading Colonials, who were merely fighting for the right to tax themselves. In

England Benjamin Franklin assured the authorities that no American, drunk or sober, had ever favored separation from the mother country; Thomas Jefferson was still "looking with fondness towards a reconciliation with Great Britain"; and George Washington told a clergyman: "If you ever hear of my joining in any such measures" (as separation) "you have my leave to set me down for everything wicked." All the larger commercial interests were strongly against any form of independence except the right to levy their own taxes, and many of them would even have preferred the victory of the Crown to the temporary interruption of trade between the two countries following an American triumph.

But there was one man who had always considered the independence of America as, sooner or later, inevitable; and though he hated war with the fervor of a Quaker and the indignation of a humanitarian, he realized, on receiving the news of Lexington, that reconciliation had also received its death volley. "I rejected the hardened, sullen-tempered Pharaoh of England for ever, and disdained the wretch, that with the pretended title of *Father of his People*, can unfeelingly hear of their slaughter, and composedly sleep with their blood upon his soul," wrote Thomas Paine.

Although the incident at Lexington was followed by a number of violent resolutions from patriotic assemblies throughout the Colonies, and although in the heat of the moment certain extremists talked about independence, Paine soon became convinced that something had to be done to clarify the situation, to unify the conflicting elements in the community, and to direct all thoughts to a single issue. He went from place to place, keeping his ears open and listening carefully to the opinions of all classes. Whenever he contributed to the discussions that raged on every side, he usually said something of note, his style of conversation being in this vein: "A greater absurdity cannot be conceived of than three millions of people running to their seacoast every time a ship arrives from London, to know what portion of liberty they should enjoy." Once he seriously annoyed his fellow-citizens by asking them to consider with what consistency or decency they complained so loudly of attempts to enslave them while they held so many thousands in slavery. This nearly got him lynched as a spy in the pay of England; but he remained unruffled and throughout the autumn of 1775 he was busily engaged in writing a pamphlet, called *Common Sense*, which he addressed to the Inhabitants of America, and which opened with these words:

"Perhaps the sentiments contained in the following pages are not *yet* sufficiently fashionable to procure them general favour; a long habit of not thinking a thing *wrong*, gives it a superficial appearance of being *right*, and raises at first a formidable outcry in defence of custom. But the tumult soon subsides. Time makes more converts than reason."

He did not think it necessary to publish his name: "Who the author of this production is, is wholly unnecessary to the public, as the object for attention is the *doctrine itself*, not the *man*."

Since "the cause of America is in a great measure the cause of all mankind," he started off with a few remarks on the origin and object of government. "Society is produced by our wants," he declared, "and government by our wickedness. . . . The first is a patron, the last a punisher. Society in every state is a blessing; but government, even in its best state, is but a necessary evil; in its worst state an intolerable one. . . . Government, like dress, is the badge of lost innocence; the palaces of kings are built on the ruins of the bowers of paradise." The design and end of all government was freedom and security.

As an Englishman he was able to tell the Americans something about the Crown and constitution of their oppressors: "The constitution of England is so exceedingly complex, that the nation may suffer for years together without being able to discover in which part the fault lies." The English had been wise enough "to shut and lock a door against absolute monarchy" but they had been foolish enough "to put the Crown in possession of the key." The fate of Charles I had only made kings more subtle, not more just.

Since he was addressing a people who believed the Bible to be the authentic word of God, he cunningly used it to prove that the Almighty was a republican at heart: "Government by kings was first introduced into the world by the heathens, from whom the children of Israel copied the custom. It was the most prosperous invention the devil ever set on foot for the promotion of idolatry. The heathen paid divine honours to their deceased kings, and the Christian world hath improved on the plan, by doing the same to its living ones. How impious is the title of sacred majesty applied to a worm, who in the midst of his splendour is crumbling into dust. . . . And when a man seriously reflects on the idolatrous homage which is paid to the persons of kings, he need not wonder that the Almighty, ever jealous of his honour, should disapprove of a form of government which so impiously invades the prerogative of Heaven. Monarchy is ranked in Scripture as one of the sins of the Jews, for which a curse in reserve is denounced against them."

Having proved his point with copious quotations from the First Book of Samuel, he pushed it farther with: "To the evil of monarchy we have added that of hereditary succession; and as the first is a degradation and lessening of ourselves, so the second, claimed as a matter of right, is an insult and imposition on posterity. . . . One of the strongest natural proofs of the folly of hereditary rights in kings is, that nature disapproves it, otherwise she would not so frequently turn it into ridicule by giving mankind an *ass for a lion*." Even the

founders of dynasties were very ordinary men and he
described the Norman Conquest in a manner that most
historians would deprecate: "A French bastard landing
with an armed banditti, and establishing himself King
of England, against the consent of the natives, is, in
plain terms, a very paltry, rascally original. It certainly
hath no divinity in it." Concluding his survey of the
rise and decline of the monarchical system, he wrote:
"In England a king hath little more to do than to make
war and give away places; which, in plain terms, is to
impoverish the nation and set it together by the ears. A
pretty business, indeed, for a man to be allowed eight
hundred thousand sterling a year for, and worshipped
into the bargain! Of more worth is one honest man to
society, and in the sight of God, than all the crowned
ruffians that ever lived." In any case the Americans already had a King, and Paine told them where to look
for him: "He reigns above, and does not make havoc
of mankind, like the Royal Brute of England."

Turning to those of his readers who were more concerned with mammon than with God, he remarked: "I
have heard it asserted by some that, as America had
flourished under her former connection with Great
Britain, the same connection is necessary towards her
future happiness, and will always have the same effect.
Nothing can be more fallacious than this kind of argument. We may as well assert that because a child has
thrived upon milk it is never to have meat, or that the

first twenty years of our lives are to become a precedent for the next twenty." He argued that America had become rich because she supplied the necessaries of life, which would always have a market while eating was the custom of Europe. "We have boasted of the protection of Great Britain, without considering that her motive was interest, not attachment. . . . The phrase *parent* or *mother country* hath been jesuitically adopted by the king and his parasites, with a low papistical design of gaining an unfair bias on the credulous weakness of our minds. . . . This new world hath been the asylum for the persecuted lovers of civil and religious liberty in every part of Europe. Hither have they fled, not from the tender embraces of the mother, but from the cruelty of the monster." Then came two phrases that have guided the policy of American statesmen from that day to this: "As Europe is our market for trade, we ought to form no partial connection with any part of it. It is the true interest of America to steer clear of European contentions. . . ."

England had carried fire and sword into her Colonies, yet many Americans still cried for reconciliation. "As well can the lover forgive the ravisher of his mistress as the Continent forgive the murderers of Britain." To such men of "passive tempers" Thomas Paine spoke clearly: "You have the heart of a coward and the spirit of a sycophant." Could they not see that England consulted the good of America only so far as it answered her own purpose? "In order to show that reconciliation now is a dangerous doctrine, I affirm that it would be policy in the King at this time to repeal the acts, for the sake of reinstating himself in the government of the provinces; in order that *he may accomplish by craft and subtlety, in the long run, what he cannot do by force and violence in the short one*. Reconciliation and ruin are nearly related."

No, they must forget all about England: "Every day wears out the little remains of kindred between us and them." From such a connection they could expect nothing but disaster. "If she is once admitted to the government of America again, this continent will not be worth living in." The untutored Indian was less a savage than the King of Britain. And now, if ever, was the time to throw off the yoke. It has been said by many that the Colonies were too young for insurrection, that they were not prepared for a war of independence, that they ought to wait another forty or fifty years. Absurd! The independence of America should have dated from "the first musket that was first fired against her." Besides, "the bravest achievements were always accomplished in the nonage of a nation. . . . The more men have to lose, the less willing they are to venture. The rich are in general slaves to fear, and submit to courtly power with the trembling duplicity of a spaniel."

But Paine appealed to the idealism of the Colonials as well as to their reason:

"The sun never shined on a cause of greater worth."

"Our plan is peace for ever."

"O! ye that love mankind! Ye that dare oppose, not only the tyranny, but the tyrant, stand forth! Every spot of the Old World is overrun with oppression. Freedom hath been hunted round the globe. Asia and Africa have long expelled her, Europe regards her like a stranger, and England hath given her warning to depart. O! receive the fugitive; and prepare in time an asylum for mankind."

"We have it in our power to begin the world over again. A situation, similar to the present, hath not happened since the days of Noah till now. The birthday of a new world is at hand, and a race of men, perhaps as numerous as all Europe contains, are to receive their portion of freedom from the event of a few months. The reflection is awful; and in this point of view, how trifling, how ridiculous, do the little paltry cavillings of a few weak or interested men appear, when weighed against the business of a world."

"Let each of us hold out to his neighbour the hearty hand of friendship, and unite in drawing a line which, like an act of oblivion, shall bury in forgetfulness every former dissension. Let the names of whig and tory be extinct; and let none other be heard among us, than those of a good citizen; an open and resolute friend; and a virtuous supporter of the RIGHTS OF MANKIND and of the FREE AND INDEPENDENT STATES OF AMERICA.

The effect of Paine's pamphlet, published on January 10, 1776, was swift and universal. Its sale was prodigious. In less than three months 120,000 copies had been sold, and Paine refused to take a penny of the profits, half of which he offered to the publisher, who ran some risk in printing such a revolutionary work, the other half being intended to purchase mittens for the troops. But the publisher, a Scottish republican named Robert Bell, collared the lot; and Paine, who ought to have made a fortune, was actually out of pocket over the venture, because he paid the printer's bill of a later and enlarged edition and the sum was never refunded. From now to the end of his life he refused to accept money for his writings on political and theological subjects. "I should lose the spirit, the pride, and the pleasure of it," he said, "were I conscious that I looked for reward." Yet he once expressed a wish never to see Pension and Paine in the same paragraph.

Naturally *Common Sense* was attacked by reactionaries and an eminent university professor was able to point out its grammatical errors; but not since the invention of printing had a work so powerfully swayed the minds of the people to whom it was addressed; nor, on looking back, can we compare anything with it for permanent influence in the affairs of men, because no other work has ever directly and simultaneously caused a revolution and united a nation. Before its publication, except by a few hotheads and republicans here and there,

# COMMON SENSE;

ADDRESSED TO THE

# INHABITANTS

OF

# AMERICA,

On the following interesting

# SUBJECTS.

I. Of the Origin and Design of Government in general, with concise Remarks on the English Constitution.

II. Of Monarchy and Hereditary Succession.

III. Thoughts on the present State of American Affairs.

IV. Of the present Ability of America, with some miscellaneous Reflections.

---

Man knows no Master save creating HEAVEN,
Or those whom choice and common good ordain.

THOMSON.

---

## PHILADELPHIA;
Printed, and Sold, by R. BELL, in Third-Street.
MDCCLXXVI.

Title page of the first American edition of "Common Sense"

the wish for a separation from England was never seriously expressed; indeed, such a measure was abhorrent to Colonial feeling. But within a few months of its appearance the Americans were practically unanimous in their desire to renounce allegiance to the Crown. George Washington talked about "the sound doctrine and unanswerable reasoning" contained in the pamphlet, and said that it was "working a wonderful change in the minds of many men." Joel Barlow, later to win distinction as a political writer, testified "that the great American cause owed as much to the pen of Paine as to the sword of Washington." Edmund Randolph, the first Attorney-General of the United States, declared that, next to George III, the Americans were indebted to Thomas Paine for their independence. And Paul Wentworth secretly informed the English Government that *Common Sense* had worked up the Colonials "to such a high temper" that separation was inevitable.

Paine's little pamphlet soon became "the political bible of the people." By the middle of 1776 most of the states had instructed their delegates in Congress to vote for independence. But the danger was not yet past. Lord Howe was empowered by the English Government to patch up a peace and the commercial interests in New York and Pennsylvania were still wavering. Paine again came to the rescue with a pamphlet in which he pointed out that a rupture with the King of England would not mean less trade with the people of England.

Thus encouraged, Congress passed the Declaration of Independence on July 4th.

William Cobbett once asserted that, whoever may have written the Declaration, Paine was its real author. This is broadly true, for the principles he had laid down were embodied in that famous manifesto and he was hand-in-glove with Thomas Jefferson while it was being drawn up. But, unfortunately, Paine's anti-slavery clause was omitted by Jefferson, because Georgia and South Carolina wanted Negro slaves and many Northerners were doing a thriving trade in them. Eighty-five years later the states which Paine had united paid in blood for what they had made in money by rejecting his advice.

## Chapter III

CRISES

WHILE the Declaration of Independence was being signed, a process which took about three months, Paine was fighting for his adopted country. He had enlisted in a division of the Flying Camp, a body of troops that could be sent at need to any part of the country. He was stationed at Fort Lee in September, 1776, where General Nathanael Greene appointed him aide-de-camp, and where he spent his spare time "wrangling about mathematical problems" with the senior officers. During the latter part of this year the American army under Washington was passing through a depressing period. The troops were poorly clothed, badly fed, scantily provided with arms, suffering from a serious shortage of ammunition, and lacking in discipline. Washington could not even count on his numbers, because enlistments were for clearly stated periods and sometimes his army was weakened on the eve of a battle by the withdrawal of large bodies of men whose terms of service had expired.

The British forces, on the other hand, were well supplied, perfectly disciplined, not liable to numerical fluctuation, and assisted by Hessian mercenaries, to say nothing of Indian scalping-parties. Washington was beaten again and again and by the end of November the whole of his army, including the author of *Common Sense*, had retreated to Newark, owing its existence more to bad weather than to good fighting.

Washington, though outwardly calm, was almost in despair. Harassed, weary, half-clad, outnumbered, the army reached Trenton on December 4th, and on the approach of the enemy crossed the Delaware three days later. Howe, the British commander, wanted to take Philadelphia and it seemed that nothing could prevent him. "Our only dependence now is upon the speedy enlistment of a new army," wrote Washington; "if this fails, I think the game will be pretty well up." No resistance to the British advance was made by the inhabitants, because they did not think their army had a chance against the well-organized troops under Howe and because they did not wish to be murdered and plundered by King George's men. In every direction the horizon was black for the Americans: wretchedness reigned in the ranks, pessimism throughout the country; an overmastering sense of impotence dulled effort and destroyed hope; the national spirit was at its lowest ebb.

But all through the nightly vigils, from Newark to Trenton and onwards beyond the Delaware, while the half-famished, half-naked, exhausted troops lay sleeping in the rain, the pen of Thomas Paine had been busy. He who had united the Americans must now inspire them with fortitude, and the first and most notable of those stirring appeals, which he called *The Crisis*, was printed in the *Pennsylvania Journal* on December 19th and immediately afterwards circulated as a pamphlet. Its opening sentence became the rallying-cry of the new republic:

"These are the times that try men's souls. The summer soldier and the sunshine patriot will, in this crisis, shrink from the service of his country; but he that stands it *now*, deserves the love and thanks of man and woman. Tyranny, like hell, is not easily conquered; yet we have this consolation with us, that the harder the conflict, the more glorious the triumph. What we obtain too cheap, we esteem too lightly: it is dearness only that gives everything its value. Heaven knows how to put a proper price upon its goods; and it would be strange indeed, if so celestial an article as Freedom should not be highly rated. Britain, with an army to enforce her tyranny, has declared that she has a right (not only to tax) but 'to bind us in all cases whatsoever,' and if being bound in that matter is not slavery, then is there not such a thing as slavery upon earth. Even the expression is impious; for so unlimited a power can belong only to God. . . .

"I have as little superstition in me as any man living, but my secret opinion has ever been, and still is, that God Almighty will not give up a people to military destruction, or leave them unsupportedly to perish, who have so earnestly and so repeatedly sought to avoid the calamities of war, by every decent method which wisdom could invent. Neither have I so much of the infidel in me, as to suppose that He has relinquished the government of the world, and given us up to the care of devils; and as I do not, I cannot see on what grounds the king of Britain can look up to heaven for help against us: a common murderer, a highwayman, or a house-breaker, has as good a pretence as he."

Following this exordium, Paine described the recent military proceedings as an eye-witness, attacked the tories whose self-interest was ruining the cause, assured the lovers of freedom that "though the flame of liberty may sometimes cease to shine, the coal can never expire," and called upon every state to give its utmost aid:

"Up and help us! lay your shoulders to the wheel; better have too much force than too little, when so great an object is at stake. Let it be told to the future world, that in the depth of winter, when nothing but hope and virtue could survive, that the city and the country, alarmed at one common danger, came forth to meet and to repulse it. Say not that thousands are gone, turn out your tens of thousands; throw not the burden of the day upon Providence, but *'show your faith by your works,'* that God may bless you. It matters not where you live, or what rank of life you hold, the evil or the blessing will reach you all. The far and the near, the home counties and the back, the rich and the poor, will suffer or rejoice alike. The heart that feels not now, is dead: the blood of his children will curse his cowardice, who shrinks back at a time when a little might have saved the whole, and made *them* happy. I love the man that can smile at trouble, that can gather strength from distress, and grow brave by reflection. 'Tis the business of little minds to shrink; but he whose heart is firm, and whose conscience approves his conduct, will pursue his principles unto death. My own line of reasoning is to myself as straight and clear as a ray of light. Not all the treasures of the world, so far as I believe, could have induced me to support an offensive war, for I think it murder; but if a thief breaks into my house, burns and destroys my property, and kills or threatens to kill me, or those that are in it, and to 'bind me in all cases whatsoever' to his absolute will, am I to suffer it? What signifies it to me, whether he who does it is a king or a common man; my countryman, or not my countryman; whether it be done by an individual villain, or an army of them? If we reason to the root of things we shall find no difference; neither can any just cause be assigned why we should punish in the one case and pardon in the other. Let them call me rebel, and welcome, I feel no concern from it; but I should suffer the misery of devils, were I to make a whore of my soul by swearing allegiance to one whose character is that of a sottish, stupid, stubborn, worthless, brutish man. I conceive likewise a horrid idea in receiving mercy from a being, who at the last day shall be shrieking to the rocks and mountains to cover him, and fleeing with terror from the orphan, the widow, and the slain of America.

"There are cases which cannot be overdone by language, and this is one. There are persons too who see not the full extent of the evil which threatens them; they solace themselves with hopes that the enemy, if he succeed, will be merciful. It is the madness of folly, to expect mercy from those who have refused to do justice; and even mercy, where conquest is the object, is only a trick of war; the cunning of the fox is as murderous as the violence of the wolf; and we ought to guard equally against both. . . . I dwell not upon the vapours of imagination: I bring reason to your ears, and in language as plain as A, B, C, hold up truth to your eyes.

"I thank God that I fear not. I see no real cause for fear. I know our situation well, and can see the way out of it. . . . By perseverance and fortitude we have the prospect of a glorious issue; by cowardice and submission, the sad choice of a variety of evils—a ravaged country—a depopulated city—habitations without safety, and slavery without hope—our homes turned into barracks and bawdy-houses for Hessians, and a future race to provide for, whose fathers we shall doubt of. Look on this picture and weep over it! and if there yet remains one thoughtless wretch who believes it not, let him suffer it unlamented."

The effect of this pamphlet was electric. It rallied and reanimated several public bodies which had previously dispersed in alarm. It brought back many soldiers who had wearied of what had seemed a useless resistance. It nerved the inhabitants of the countryside to put every obstacle in the path of the invaders. It aroused enthusiasm in the towns and sent up the rate of recruitment with a bound. Certain scholars triumphantly convicted Paine of error in one of his historical dates; but George Washington, who confessed his "lively sense of the importance" of Paine's works, ordered it to be read throughout the camp, and the soldiers who before had murmured of defeat were now buoyed up with a certainty of victory. Careless of historical accuracy, but alive to the urgency of Paine's words, they attacked and captured the Hessians at Trenton, a victory which turned the tide of the campaign, and a few days later they beat the army of Lord Cornwallis at Princeton.

Within a month a second *Crisis* came from the press. It took the form of a reply to Lord Howe, who had published a Proclamation granting mercy to the Americans if they would behave themselves for the future and acknowledge their sovereign lord, King George III. In this *Crisis*, dated from Philadelphia, January 13, 1777, appeared for the first time a title which has since achieved the renown its author prophesied, and Thomas Paine christened a nation when he wrote: "The UNITED STATES OF AMERICA will sound as pompously in the world or in history as the Kingdom of Great Britain."

The one-time stay-maker opened his address to (and dressing-down of) the noble viscount with some pride:

"Universal empire is the prerogative of a writer. His concerns are with all mankind, and though he cannot command their obedience, he can assign them their duty. The Republic of Letters is more ancient than monarchy, and of far higher character in the world than the vassal court of Britain; he that rebels against reason is a real rebel, but he that in defence of reason rebels against tyranny, has a better title to 'Defender of the Faith' than George the third."

Howe was reminded of the brutal behavior of the British generals: "The only instance of justice, if it can be called such, which has distinguished you for impartiality, is that you treated and plundered all alike." But now that the English were beginning to taste of defeat they were retiring on the towns and sending home bulletins of conquered territory: "You have managed your Jersey expedition so very dexterously, that the dead only are conquerors, because none will dispute the ground with them." Paine admitted that there had been a certain lukewarmness among portions of the American population: "Some men have naturally a military turn, and can brave hardships and the risk of life with a cheerful face; others have not; no slavery appears to them so great as the fatigue of arms, and no terror so powerful as that of personal danger. What can we say? We cannot alter nature, neither ought we to punish the son because the father begot him in a cowardly mood. However, I believe most men have more courage than they know of, and that a little at first is enough to begin with. I knew the time when I thought the whistling of a cannon ball would have frightened me almost to death; but I have since tried it, and find that I can stand it with as little discomposure, and, I believe, with a much easier conscience than your lordship. The same dread would return to me again were I in your situation, for my solemn belief of your cause is, that it is hellish and damnable, and, under that conviction, every thinking man's heart *must* fail him."

Howe would learn in time that the British forces could never hope to win the war: "Englishmen always travel for knowledge, and your lordship, I hope, will return, if you return at all, much wiser than you came." The Americans would never give in because "What we contend for is worthy the affliction we may go through," and "what are the inconveniences of a few months to the tributary bondage of ages?" Paine also delivered a serious warning: " 'Tis the unhappy temper of the English to be pleased with any war, right or wrong, be it but successful; but they soon grow discontented with ill-fortune, and it is an even chance that they are as clamorous for peace next summer, as the king and his ministers were for war last winter." Besides, what good would it do England if she were to conquer America? "I wish as well to the true prosperity of England as you can, but I consider INDEPENDENCE America's natural right and interest, and never could see any real disservice it would be to Britain. If an English merchant receives an order, and is paid for it, it signifies nothing to him who governs the country." In case Howe should criticize his style or sentiments, Paine observed: "What I write is pure nature, and my pen and my soul have ever gone together."

Having strongly advised Howe to pack up and return to his sovereign lord without loss of time, and having warned him that England's chances of making an honorable peace with America were rapidly vanishing, Paine turned his attention to the Quakers, devoting his third *Crisis* to them. The Quakers of Philadelphia had recently issued a "testimony" of their loyalty to the English monarchy. "These men are continually harping on the great sin of *our* bearing arms," said Paine, "but the king of Britain may lay waste the world in blood and famine, and they, poor fallen souls, have nothing to say." He recapitulated the points in favor of independence, asserted that "either we or Britain are absolutely right or absolutely wrong through the whole," described the denial of their right to independence as "a kind of atheism against nature," and asked, "Is it the interest of a man to be a boy all his life?" England was fighting this war because she was jealous of America: "She began to view this country with the same uneasy, malicious eye with which a covetous guardian would view his ward, whose estate he had been enriching himself by for twenty years, and saw him just arriving at manhood." However, this was all to the good: "Good heavens! what volumes of thanks does America owe to Britain! What infinite obligation to the tool that fills, with paradoxical vacancy, the throne! Nothing but the sharpest essence of villainy, compounded with the strongest distillation of folly, could have produced a menstruum that would have effected a separation." America had come of age in the conflict: "Truly may we say that never did men grow old in so short a time! We have crowded the business of an age into the compass of a few months." Soon America would "exchange Britain for Europe—shake hands with the world—live at peace with the world—and trade to any market where we can buy and sell."

But the enemy was not yet beaten: "Britain, like a gamester nearly ruined, hath now put all her losses into one bet, and is playing a desperate game for the total. If she wins it, she wins from me my life." The King's troops must be kept in check for a reasonable period, then victory was bound to follow: "Like a wounded disabled whale, they want only time and room to die in; and though in the agony of their exit it may be unsafe to live within the flapping of their tail, yet every hour shortens their date, and lessens their power of mischief."

Of wars in Europe Paine had this to say: "The spirit of duelling, extended on a national scale, is a proper character for European wars. They have seldom any other motive than pride, or any other object than fame. The conquerors and the conquered are generally ruined alike, and the chief difference at last is, that the one marches home with his honours, and the other without them. 'Tis the natural temper of the English to fight for a feather, if they suppose *that feather* to be an affront. . . ."

Their worst enemy was the tory within the gates: "It is remarkable that the whole race of prostitutes in New York were tories; and the schemes for supporting the tory cause in this city, for which several are now in jail, and one hanged, were concerted and carried on in common bawdy-houses, assisted by those who kept them."

Another enemy to the cause of independence was "the present race of Quakers. They have artfully changed themselves into a different sort of people to what they used to be, and yet have the address to persuade each other that they are not altered; like antiquated virgins, they see not the havoc deformity has made upon them, but pleasantly mistaking wrinkles for dimples, conceive themselves yet lovely and wonder at the stupid world for not admiring them." Paine did not mince matters. Referring to the famous Quakeress, Hannah Lightfoot, and her putative husband, Axford, then resident in Philadelphia, he wrote: "If a Quaker, in defence of his just rights, his property, and the chastity of his house, takes up a musket, he is expelled the meeting; but the present king of England, who seduced and took into keeping a sister of their society, is reverenced and supported by repeated Testimonies, while the friendly noodle from whom she was taken (and who is now in this city) continues a drudge in the service of his rival, as if proud of being cuckolded by a creature called a king."

Paine concluded his pamphlet with a suggestion that anyone who refused to fight against Great Britain should be heavily taxed, the patriot who risked his life and property to reap the full benefit of such taxation.

After the engagements at Trenton and Princeton there was a lull in the hostilities. Paine, though still on General Greene's staff, was busy writing his pamphlets, and in April, 1776, Congress appointed him secretary to the Committee for Foreign Affairs at a nominal salary of seventy dollars a month, an actual salary of fifteen. Few Foreign Secretaries nowadays would be willing to work for £36 a year. His appointment was opposed in quarters where his views on Negro slavery were unpopular, but his public services had been such that some sort of recognition had to be made. Later he was made to suffer for having dared to oppose the vested interest in human flesh and blood.

The year 1777 was passed in much anxiety. Paine was engaged by the Pennsylvanian Assembly to keep them fully advised of the movements of Washington's army; and as he was also in constant correspondence with foreign agents and leading members of Congress, his hands were full. He made great efforts to get the military authorities in Philadelphia to defend it against the British, but they lacked his enthusiasm and the enemy occupied the city in September of that year. Washington's failure to save it was compared with the success of General Gates, to whom Burgoyne had surrendered, and Congress was full of intrigues against the commander-in-chief, who was with his ill-equipped army at Valley Forge. Paine was there, too, and we hear of him taking part in several dangerous exploits. He was sent by Greene to bring news from Fort Mifflin, which was being bombarded by the entire British fleet, and for some hours he was at the mercy of the enemy's batteries in an open boat. Alone he reconnoitered the English pickets in the neighborhood of Philadelphia. And he volunteered to lead a small party down the river to set fire to the English fleet, an offer that was declined by the naval commander at Trenton.

By the winter of 1777 a sort of military stalemate had been reached and dissatisfaction and intrigue were rife among the Americans. Wishing to inspirit his countrymen, Paine turned from his military and secretarial duties to write another *Crisis*, which he addressed to the British general, Sir William Howe, then in possession of Philadelphia. After trouncing him for encouraging "the forging and uttering of counterfeit continental bills," an act for which "the laws of any civilised country would condemn you to the gibbet without regard to your rank or titles," Paine described his military maneuvers in language that must have irritated Howe far more than being accused of felony: "You have moved in and out, backwards and forwards, round and round, as if valor consisted in a military jig. The history and figure of your movements would be truly ridiculous could they be justly delineated. They resemble the labors of a puppy pursuing his tail; the end is still at the same distance, and all the turnings round must be done over again." Then it was the turn of Howe's employers: "There is not in the compass of language a sufficiency of words to express the baseness of your king, his ministry and his army. They have refined upon villainy till it wants a name. To the fiercer vices of former ages they have added the dregs and scummings of the most finished rascality, and are so completely sunk in serpentine deceit, that there is not left among them *one* generous enemy." Then of Howe's country: "Extent of dominion has been her ruin, and instead of civilizing others has brutalized herself."

But what could be said of war-makers in general? Paine said it:

"If there is a sin superior to every other, it is that of wilful and offensive war. . . . He who is the author of a war, lets loose the whole contagion of hell, and opens a vein that bleeds a nation to death. . . . When we take a survey of mankind, we cannot help cursing the wretch who, to the unavoidable misfortunes of nature, shall wilfully add the calamities of war. One would think there were evils enough in the world without studying to increase them, and that life is sufficiently short without shaking the sand that measures it. The histories of Alexander, and Charles of Sweden, are the histories of human devils; a good man cannot think of their actions without abhorrence, nor of their deaths without rejoicing. To see the bounties of heaven destroyed, the beautiful face of nature laid waste, and the choicest works of creation and art tumbled into ruin, would fetch a curse from the soul of piety itself."

In nearly every number of *The Crisis* it is possible to feel the urgency and momentum of those strenuous days. Odd phrases seem to leap from the printed page and hit the ear like the note of a bell:

"He that can conquer finds his mind too free and pleasant to be brutish; and he that intends to conquer never makes too much show of his strength."

"Those who expect to reap the blessings of freedom, must, like men, undergo the fatigues of supporting it."

"The nearer any disease approaches to a crisis, the nearer it is to a cure. Danger and deliverance make their advances together, and it is only the last push, in which one or the other takes the lead."

"It is only those that are not in action, that feel languor and heaviness, and the best way to rub it off is to turn out, and make sure work of it."

"We fight not to enslave, but to set a country free, and to make room upon the earth for honest men to live in."

"What we have now to do is as clear as light, and the way to do it as straight as a line."

Unfortunately it was not so clear as light to the commercial interests in the larger towns; and when, following a treaty between France and America and the evacuation of Philadelphia by the British, a commission was sent out from England to gain by guile what she had failed to win by force, Paine had to expose the trickery of the tories in a *Crisis* addressed to the British Commissioners, who were told: "Like men in a state of intoxication, you forget that the rest of the world have eyes, and that the same stupidity which conceals you from yourselves exposes you to their satire and contempt." It was vitally necessary to speak plainly because in New York, Boston, and Philadelphia, quite apart from the trading connections between leading houses and British firms, reaction had set in and people were beginning to wonder whether popular government would, after all, be such a blessing. And so, to place the matter in its clearest light, Paine wrote another *Crisis* for the benefit of "The People of England," explaining why it came about that they had been dragged into the war, and how, by substituting democratic for monarchical government, they could extricate themselves from a false position and henceforth live at peace with their neighbors and kinsmen. Britain, said he, coining a phrase that has since been frequently misused, Britain "has made war like an Indian against the religion of humanity." Well over a century after it was given, England took one piece of advice which Paine tendered her in this pamphlet and granted self-government to her colonies:

"The title which she assumed, of parent country, led to, and pointed out the propriety, wisdom and advantage of a separation; for, as in private life, children grow into men, and by setting up for themselves, extend and secure the interest of the whole family, so in the settlement of colonies large enough to admit of maturity, the same policy should be pursued, and the same consequences would follow. Nothing hurts the affections both of parents and children so much, as living too closely connected, and keeping up the distinction too long. . . .

"When you saw the state of strength and opulence, and that by her own industry, which America had arrived at, you ought to have advised her to set up for herself, and proposed an alliance of interest with her, and in so doing you would have drawn, and that at her own expense, more real advantage, and more military supplies and assistance, both of ships and men, than from any weak and wrangling government that you could exercise over her. In short, had you studied only the domestic politics of a family, you would have learned how to govern the state."

Every number of *The Crisis* had a considerable effect on popular opinion, because it spoke for the man in the street, or rather for the man in the field, and each issue was sold in tens of thousands. Paine, though sometimes he could not afford to pay for his boots, refused to benefit from the sale of his books. No one had ever sacrificed more in the cause of liberty, and soon he was to make the final sacrifice. He must have been aware, for he was shrewd enough in everyday matters, that every time he attacked the American tories he was antagonizing some of their tools in Congress. Yet such was the simplicity of his nature that he believed in the eventual triumph of truth, such the singleness of his purpose that he never veered from his course but kept on "as straight as a line." There is a verse in one of his poems (*The American Patriot's Prayer*) which may have sprung from some foreboding of his own fate:

> Let me not faction's partial hate
>   Pursue to this Land's woe;
> Nor grasp the thunder of the state
>   To wound a private foe.

## Chapter IV

---

### UPS AND DOWNS

---

IT WAS only natural that America should look to France for help in the war against England, because only a few years before the struggle commenced the French had been driven out of Canada and India by the English. There was, however, a treaty between the two European powers which Louis XVI did not wish to break, and he could not assist the Americans without practically declaring war against England. His Minister, Vergennes, was not so scrupulous, and saw a way of hurting their hated competitor without serious risk to themselves.

There was at the French court a certain Monsieur de Beaumarchais, who was quite willing to lend himself to any scheme that might put money in his pocket. Beaumarchais, with the assistance of Mozart, is now famous as the creator of "Figaro"; but in those days he was chiefly known as a courtier with a clever tongue, a guitar-player with a nimble touch, and a man of affairs with a shrewd eye to business. At the instigation of Vergennes he laid a proposal before the king. It was written with considerable cunning. The king was reminded of the indignities to which France had been subjected, of the necessity of retrieving the national honor. There was but one way of avenging the wrongs that England had heaped upon her: by helping the Americans to prolong the war and thus depleting the financial resources of Great Britain. How was this to be done? Clearly not by means of a government loan, for that would result in open war; but under cover of a commercial transaction. One million livres was to be handed over to Beaumarchais, who would then arrange that half of it should reach America in gold and the other half in powder. Beaumarchais did not think it necessary to emphasize the fact that he would pocket a large profit on the difference between the price of powder in France and its estimated value on reaching America; or that, in order to make the business appear like a trading agreement, he intended to benefit handsomely by large consignments of tobacco from America. It took the king about a year to reach a decision; but when the queen's influence came into play, he gave in, writing *"Bon"* on Beaumarchais' receipt for the million livres. This was in June, 1776.

A month later a gentleman named Silas Deane arrived in Paris. As the commercial agent appointed by Congress to purchase munitions in France, he was informed by Arthur Lee, secret agent for Virginia in London, that Beaumarchais had received the million livres as a gift from the French Government. Deane at once got into touch with Beaumarchais, who flatly denied this, but said that he had been empowered to supply America with powder, etc., in exchange for tobacco and cash. Beaumarchais backed his denial with a number of cash payments to Deane, who naturally accepted the word of so generous a man in preference to that of Lee, who was not in a position to substantiate his assertion with financial assistance. Deane therefore signed a contract with a comic-opera firm named Roderique Hortalez & Co., invented by Beaumarchais to cover his interesting transactions, binding the United States to make the necessary exchange of commodities within six months and to repay the balance in a year. At the hint, no doubt, of certain disaffected members of Congress, Deane then entered into negotiations with some German prince who might be needed to supersede Washington as commander-in-chief of the American forces and whose presence in the States would be useful if at any time the Americans decided to have a king of their own. Meanwhile Beaumarchais dispatched three ships loaded with war material to America, of which two were captured and one arrived safely.

Six months after the arrival of Deane in France, Congress sent two more representatives to Paris, Franklin and Lee, in order to arrange an alliance between the

countries. The French Government, anxious to obtain
commercial concessions from America, told their visitors
that the money handed over to Beaumarchais had been
a royal gift, for which no return would be expected.
This fact was made known to Congress while it was considering a claim from Beaumarchais (backed by Deane)
for payment of goods supplied by the Figaro firm.
There appeared to be a misunderstanding somewhere
and Deane was recalled to clarify the situation. He was
called twice before Congress, but failed to give a reasonable explanation of his conduct. It came out that he had
received certain sums from Beaumarchais for "personal
expenses," and he was unable to produce vouchers for
his contracts. The whole business seemed extremely
fishy and Congress refused him a third hearing. Whereupon he lost his temper and attacked the honesty of
Congress in the press, claiming personal credit for having raised the "loan" and for pretty well everything else
that had been done before and since he went to France.

This was altogether too much for Thomas Paine,
who as Foreign Secretary had been privily advised of
all the proceedings and knew from Lee that the money
was a gift, not a loan. Being one of the very few famous
men in history whose patriotism was wholly uninflu-
enced by his pocket, he saw Deane simply as a black-
guard who was "on the make"; he was seriously alarmed
about the effect on the people of Deane's onslaught
upon Congress; and, as a thorough republican, he was

furious with Deane for having negotiated with German royalty for a successor to Washington. "His life has been fraud," wrote Paine at a later date, "and his character is that of a plodding, plotting, cringing mercenary, capable of any disguise that suited his purpose." In order to set the public mind at rest, since a meeting to demand justice for Deane had actually been arranged, Paine replied in the press, defending the honor of Congress and giving all the relevant facts. He said that the supplies had been arranged "as a present" long before Deane's arrival in France. Unfortunately, his statement proved that the present was made by the king before an alliance was signed between the two governments, and as there was then a treaty between France and England this reflected seriously on the honor of Louis XVI. Naturally the French minister in America, Gérard, had to lodge a complaint, which he did with the more vigor because he himself was financially interested in the claim of Beaumarchais.

Somehow, for the sake of the alliance between France and America, Congress had to disown Paine and brand him, officially, as a liar. The situation would have been simple enough if he had been of a pliable nature. No one but Paine, certainly no politician, would have experienced the least difficulty in finding a formula to cover his indiscretion and turn it to his advantage. But Paine was Paine and Congress knew it; knew it so well that already there were many members who would have seized any opportunity to get rid of so inconveniently honest a man. Moreover the President, John Jay, and several others were friends of Deane's. Congress therefore acted with commendable promptitude. Paine was called before the House in secret session on January 6, 1779, and was asked one question: Was he the author of the articles, signed "Common Sense," in which such-and-such had appeared? "Yes," he replied, and before another word could be spoken he was told to withdraw. Any further questions, and especially any further answers, would have been risky.

Paine then wrote a memorial to Congress, begging to know whether there was any charge against him, and, if so, claiming the right to answer it in person: "I make my application to the heart of every gentleman in this House, that, before he decides on a point that may affect my reputation, he will duly consider his own. . . . I have no favour to ask more than to be candidly and honourably dealt by." But the last thing in the world desired by Congress at that moment was the candid and honorable treatment of Paine, because such treatment would have let the cat out of the bag; and although a vote for his dismissal from office was defeated by one, the mere fact that his character could be made the subject of such a vote had the effect that his enemies in Congress knew it would have. He resigned.

Thereafter it was sedulously spread abroad that he had broken his oath of office; but as his oath only bound him to secrecy concerning matters which he should be "directed to keep secret," the accusation was groundless. Paine continued to address letters to Congress: "I have betrayed no Trust," he declared, "because I have constantly employed that Trust to the public good. I have revealed no secrets because I have told nothing that was, or I conceive ought to be a secret." He reminded Congress that "they began their hard treatment of me while I was defending their injured and insulted honor," and consoled himself with the reflection that "as I came into office an honest man, I go out of it with the same character." His letters were suppressed and ignored.

Meanwhile Gérard, the French minister, had been trying to persuade Paine to recant. After all, Paine's position in America was considerable. "You know too well," wrote Gérard to Vergennes, "the prodigious effects produced by the writings of this famous personage among the people of the States to cause me any fear of your disapproval of my resolution." His resolution was simple and would have been effective with almost anyone but Paine, to whom he had offered a bribe (or, as he put it, "a salary in the king's name" of about £700 a year) on condition that the author of *Common Sense* should publish nothing on political affairs, nor on Congress, without consulting him, but should henceforth devote his pen to the propagation of sentiments favorable to the French alliance. Paine replied, through an intermediary, that any service he could render to either

of the countries in alliance, or to both, he had always
done and would always continue to do, but that "Mr.
Gérard's *esteem* will be the only compensation I shall
desire." It was, of course, impossible to do business with
a man who preferred esteem to cash, especially as Paine
published a circumstantial account of Gérard's offer in
the press, and the French minister had to fall back on
more accommodating scribes, who under the pseudonyms of "Honest Politician" and "Americanus" did all
that was required of them.

Although not concerned with our subject, it is interesting to note at this point that the fates of Beaumarchais
and Deane were consonant with the best traditions of
copybook morality. The former, though quick enough
to elude the guillotine, was not clever enough to buy
securities in less impulsive countries than France, and
died a pauper in Holland. The latter, though cunning
enough to become pro-British when he returned to Europe, was not cute enough to realize he was backing a
loser, and died a pauper in England. Their fates, however, should not be used as warnings to the young. As
a general rule it is the Beaumarchais of life who ends in
the Upper House, the Paine in the workhouse; and,
indeed, though the times were against Beaumarchais and
Deane, their descendants profited by their duplicity; for
the claims of both financial experts, bequeathed to their
children, were eventually paid by the governments of
France and America.

For Paine, from the moment he resigned office, there commenced a period of extreme perturbation. Nearly everyone thought him wrong in exposing Deane, and "the best friends I then had," he complained, "stood at a distance." It was the first serious step towards his ultimate disillusionment. "I prevented Deane's fraudulent demand being paid, and so far the country is obliged to me, but I became the victim of my integrity." A simple and truthful explanation, but he had not arrived at the point when he could see that the fault was his for expecting too much of human nature. He was yet to learn that human beings are not at their best when on a committee, that the representatives of mankind represent the greed, not the generosity, of individual men. At first his treatment by Congress exasperated him and he declared in the press that as he was the only honest man employed in American affairs he should be given authority to purify Congress; but as no power but Congress could grant him such authority, it remained unpurified. He was now existing on a pittance earned as a clerk in a law office; in spite of which his pen remained busy in the common good, writing a number of articles which claimed the right of America to the Newfoundland fisheries. This dispute was settled 130 years later.

Paine's position throughout the greater part of 1779 was acutely uncomfortable. From being a statesman at the center of affairs he had become an office drudge. He was ridiculed in the press and jeered at in public. One

day a party of gentlemen, excited by wine, met him in
the street and on patriotic grounds tripped him into the
gutter. This was afterwards used as evidence that Paine
had been drinking too much. The ingratitude of the
country and the antagonism of his friends preyed upon
his mind; he seldom went out, for he could not afford
to hire a horse, and "a sedentary life cannot be supported without jolting exercise"; he was even too poor
to buy enough food to keep him in health. Illness fell
upon him at regular intervals and he realized that "unless I alter my way of life, it will alter me."

To save himself from a lingering death and to recover, if possible, his lost reputation, he was driven
to a decision which, for one of his proud nature, must
have caused him many miserable hours. This was to
issue for his personal benefit a collected edition of his
works, and to write a history of the Revolution; but as
he did not like to raise a subscription for these publications until he could make sure of getting the paper
(from France) on which to print them, he wrote first to
his friend Henry Laurens, who had formerly been
President of Congress and who alone remained his
friend after the Deane affair, and then to the Executive
Council of Pennsylvania, explaining the circumstances
and suggesting a loan on which he could pay his way
until the two volumes of his Works were ready for
issue. As he had once slaved for the Pennsylvania Assembly without a farthing's remuneration, he added that

if the loan were refused some compensation might be
made him for past services. The Executive Council,
nervous of the French minister, asked Gérard whether
he had any objection to the official employment of
Paine. Seemingly under the impression that a govern-
mental job was equivalent to a bribe, Gérard wished the
Council better luck than had attended his own efforts
to induce Paine "to direct his pen in a way useful to the
public welfare." Paine was elected Clerk to the Pennsylvania Assembly in November, 1779, and in that capacity wrote the first proclamation of Negro emancipation in America when an act for the abolition of slavery
in Pennsylvania was brought in.

In the year 1780 he wrote three more numbers of
*The Crisis*. The scene of war had been shifted to the
south, where the enemy were for a time victorious,
Charleston and Savannah falling into the hands of King
George. In the north nothing was happening. General
Clinton had occupied New York and Washington had
taken up a position at White Plains near by. The two
forces then "watched" one another for about three
years. The English thoroughly enjoyed themselves;
they were comfortably housed, supplies were plentiful,
and the brothels in New York did a thriving trade. The
Americans, on the other hand, were demoralized by inactivity, by lack of provisions, by cheerless quarters, and
not least by the invitation, distributed in leaflets by the
enemy, that they should partake of the pleasures in the

city. Washington reported "mutiny and sedition" among his men, upon which Paine started a subscription for the relief of the troops, heading it with five hundred dollars of his hard-earned pay. His example, backed by another *Crisis*, was speedily followed. A sum of £300,000 was raised, a bank was opened, the army was supplied with necessaries, the disaffection subsided—and Paine was made a Master of Arts by the Pennsylvania University.

Having tided over the financial difficulties of the moment with a *Crisis* on the subject of taxation, and having antagonized Virginia by asserting the Federal right to certain territories claimed by that state, Paine sailed for France early in 1781. For some time he had felt that he would be of greater service to his country in Europe than in America, and a few months before his departure he had suggested to General Nathanael Greene that he should go secretly to England in order to use the press, which he called "the tongue of the world," to popularize the idea of American independence. To achieve this end he would have employed the subtle method of apologizing for the errors of the British nation, instead of attacking them, and thus "accommodating the measure to their pride." He had fully realized the danger of such a course: "I have everything to apprehend should I fall into their hands." But as he had "had a considerable share in promoting the Declaration of Independence in this country," he wished "to be a means of promoting the acknowledgment of it in that." The plan came to nothing and a few months afterwards his services were required in France.

Congress wanted eight million dollars; failing which the war could not be carried on. On the advice of Paine it was decided that the French Government should be asked to help and Colonel John Laurens was appointed to negotiate a loan. Laurens said he would go if Paine went with him; so Paine put aside the history of the Revolution for which he had been collecting materials and again helped to make history instead of writing it. They reached France in March, 1781. It was as well that Laurens had insisted on Paine's company, because the colonel nearly wrecked the business by his enthusiasm, while the clerk brought it off by his diplomacy. The king liked Paine, was extremely pleasant to him, and the visit was a great success. They returned to America in August with two and a half million livres and a shipload of stores and clothing. Washington had been waiting on tenterhooks for the safe arrival of money and material, and as a direct consequence of it he was able to prosecute the campaign which ended with the surrender of Cornwallis in Virginia.

In order to make this journey, so vital to the cause of American freedom, Paine had sacrificed a good job, risked his life (for capture by the British would have meant the gallows), and paid his own expenses. The colonel got all the kudos. Paine was not even thanked and was shortly so hard up that again he could not pay for the mending of a pair of boots. Fresh from the victory of Yorktown, Washington came to receive the congratulations of Congress at Philadelphia. In desperation Paine wrote him a letter, dated November 30, 1781, from "Second Street, opposite the Quaker Meeting-house": "It is seven years, *this day*, since I arrived in America, and tho' I consider them as the most honorary time of my life, they have nevertheless been the most inconvenient and even distressing. From an anxiety to support, as far as laid in my power, the reputation of the Cause of America, as well as the Cause itself, I declined the customary profits which authors are. entitled to, and I have always continued to do so; yet I never thought (if I thought at all on the matter) but that as I dealt generously and honorably by America, she would deal the same by me. But I have experienced the contrary—and it gives me much concern, not only on account of the inconvenience it has occasioned me, but because it unpleasantly lessens my opinion of the character of a country which once appeared so fair, and it hurts my mind to see her so cold and inattentive to matters which affect her reputation. . . . Wherever I go I find respect, and everybody I meet treats me with friendship; all join in censuring the neglect and throwing blame on each other, so that their civility disarms me as much as their conduct distresses me. . . . There is something peculiarly hard that the country which ought to have been to me a home has scarcely afforded me an asylum." It was his design, he said, to go to France or Holland, because "I am sure I cannot experience worse fortune than I have here."

Washington was helpful and in a few weeks Paine was offered eight hundred dollars a year for continuing to employ his pen in the common cause. Another *Crisis*, largely dealing with taxation, appeared in March, 1782, and in it Paine stressed the vital importance of the Union of the States, the supremacy of the Federal Government: "Each state is to the United States what each individual is to the state he lives in. And it is on this grand point, this movement upon one centre, that our existence as a nation, our happiness as a people, and our safety as individuals, depend." This doctrine added to its author's unpopularity in many quarters because the various states were jealous of their rights and had not begun to think nationally. As in so many other respects, Paine was long before his time.

Two months later, having discussed the matter with Washington over "a crust of bread and cheese" in his own lodgings, Paine produced another *Crisis*. England had been doing her best to break the alliance between America and France by making advantageous offers to each in turn. "Let the world and Britain know that we are neither to be bought nor sold," declared Paine, adding, however, a warning: "We are a young nation, just stepping upon the stage of public life, and the eye of the world is upon us to see how we act." Did England really believe that she could win by perfidy what she had lost by brutality? "Men are often hurt by a mean action who are not startled at a wicked one." Fortunately, England's behavior in the past had prepared them for any emergency. "That a country has a right to be as foolish as it pleases, has been proved by the practice of England for many years past," he said on another occasion. Now he explained the normal procedure: "On our part, in order to know, at any time, what the British Government will do, we have only to find out what they ought *not* to do, and this last will be their conduct. . . . Every campaign has added to their loss, and every year to their disgrace: till unable to go on, and ashamed to go back, their politics have come to a halt, and all their fine prospects to a halter." No words could express the feelings of every decent man at the latest example of British turpitude:

"We sometimes experience sensations to which language is not equal. The conception is too bulky to be born alive, and in the torture of thinking, we stand dumb. Our feelings, imprisoned by their magnitude, find no way out—and, in the struggle of expression, every finger tries to be a tongue. The machinery of the body seems too little for the mind, and we look about for helps to show our thoughts by. Such must be the sensation of America, whenever Britain, teeming with corruption, shall propose to her to sacrifice her faith."

In the autumn of 1782 appeared a *Crisis* addressed to

the Earl of Shelburne (afterwards Lord Lansdowne), who had stated that the independence of America would be the ruin of England. "Is the case so strangely altered, that those who once thought we could not live without them, are now brought to declare that they cannot exist without us?" asked Paine, who also pointed out that "the guilt of a government is the crime of a whole country," and that, as usual, the poor would pay for the follies of the rich: "The British army in America care not how long the war lasts. They enjoy an easy and indolent life. They fatten on the folly of one country and the spoils of another; and, between their plunder and their pay, may go home rich. But the case is very different with the labouring farmer, the working tradesman, and the necessitous poor in England, the sweat of whose brow goes day after day to feed, in prodigality and sloth, the army that is robbing both them and us."

But indeed there could be no real understanding between England and America: "We are a people who think not as you think; and what is equally true, you cannot feel as we feel. The situations of the two countries are exceedingly different. Ours has been the seat of war; yours has seen nothing of it. The most wanton destruction has been committed in our sight; the most insolent barbarity has been acted on our feelings. We can look round and see the remains of burnt and destroyed houses, once the fair fruit of hard industry, and now the striking monuments of British brutality. We walk over the dead whom we loved, in every part of America, and remember by whom they fell. There is scarcely a village but brings to life some melancholy thought, and reminds us of what we have suffered, and of those we have lost by the inhumanity of Britain. A thousand images arise to us, which, from situation, you cannot see, and are accompanied by as many ideas which you cannot know; and therefore your supposed system of reasoning would apply to nothing, and all your expectations die of themselves."

In April, 1783, the war came to an end and Paine published his last *Crisis*. " 'The times that tried men's souls' are over," he began, "and the greatest and completest revolution the world ever knew, gloriously and happily accomplished." But now was the real testing-time for America: "Let, then, the world see that she can bear prosperity: and that her honest virtue in time of peace, is equal to the bravest virtue in time of war." No nation ever had such opportunities: "To see it in our power to make a world happy—to teach mankind the art of being so—to exhibit, on the theatre of the universe, a character hitherto unknown—and to have, as it were, a new creation intrusted to our hands, are honours that command reflection, and can neither be too highly estimated, nor too gratefully received." Again he warned his countrymen that everything depended on the absolute sovereignty of the United States: "But that which must more forcibly strike a thoughtful, penetrating mind, and which includes and renders easy all inferior concerns, is the *Union of the States*. On this our great national character depends. It is this which must give us importance abroad and security at home."

He closed on a personal note:

"It was the cause of America that made me an author. The force with which it struck my mind, and the dangerous condition the country appeared to me in, by courting an impossible and an unnatural reconciliation with those who were determined to reduce her, instead of striking out into the only line that could cement and save her, A DECLARATION OF INDEPENDENCE, made it impossible for me, feeling as I did, to be silent; and if, in the course of more than seven years, I have rendered her any service, I have likewise added something to the reputation of literature, by freely and disinterestedly employing it in the great cause of mankind, and showing that there may be genius without prostitution. . . .

"But as the scenes of war are closed, and every man preparing for home and happier times, I therefore take my leave of the subject. I have most sincerely followed it from beginning to end, and through all its turns and windings; and whatever country I may hereafter be in, I shall always feel an honest pride at the part I have taken and acted, and a gratitude to nature and providence for putting it in my power to be of some use to mankind."

## Chapter V

### PERSONAL

WITH the end of the war there was an end of Paine's salary and the autumn of 1783 found him living in a small house at Bordentown, New Jersey, close to his friend, Colonel Kirkbride, by whose side he had fought and with whom he had helped to draw up the Constitution of Pennsylvania. They were both tremendously keen on scientific experiments and just now Paine was full of mechanical inventions, spending much time over the model of a bridge. His chief wish at this period was to settle down to a life of scientific inquiry, but before doing so he wanted to revisit England and see his parents and friends once more.

Again he was enduring the humiliation and irritation of poverty. A few friends were only too anxious to help. Colonel Laurens invited him to visit Carolina: "You will be received with open arms and all that affection and respect which our citizens are anxious to testify to the author of *Common Sense* and *The Crisis.* . . . I wish you to regard this part of America as your particular home—and everything that I can command in it to be in common between us." General Nathanael Greene also wrote from Carolina: "Many people wish to get you into this country. I see you are determined to follow your genius and not your fortune. I have always been in hopes that Congress would have made some handsome acknowledgment to you for past services. I must confess that I think you have been shamefully neglected; and that America is indebted to few characters more than to you. But as your passion leads to fame, and not to wealth, your mortification will be the less. Your fame for your writings will be immortal. At present my expenses are great; nevertheless, if you are not conveniently situated, I shall take a pride and pleasure in contributing all in my power to render your situation happy." But if friends were kind the politicians were cold, and as private benefactions were not to his taste he wrote, on the advice of another friend, to the President of Congress suggesting that his past services, freely given, should be considered.

In September, 1783, Washington was receiving what practically amounted to divine honors from Congress. He was installed in a mansion at Rocky Hill in order to be near Congress, then in session at Princeton, and he was living in an atmosphere of gayety and glory. There was talk of an Egyptian statue to the conqueror, of many other tributes in stone, and even of a city to be named after the savior of his country. Such was the prevailing excitement and enthusiasm that people mistook his platitudes for wit, and it says much for the General that he never once mistook himself for God. In fact, he remembered in his hour of greatness the man who had made that hour great. "I have learned since I have been at this place," wrote Washington to Paine, "that you are at Bordentown. Whether for the sake of retirement or economy, I know not. Be it for either, for both, or whatever it may, if you will come to this place, and partake with me, I shall be exceedingly happy to see you. Your presence may remind Congress of your past services to this country; and if it is in my power to impress them, command my best services with freedom, as they will be rendered cheerfully by one who entertains a lively sense of the importance of your works, and who, with much pleasure, subscribes himself, Your sincere friend."

Paine replied gratefully, accepting the invitation, and telling Washington about his letter to Congress: "I am hurt by the neglect of the collective ostensible body of America, in a way which it is probable they do not perceive my feelings. It has an effect in putting either my reputation or their generosity at stake; for it cannot fail of suggesting that either I (notwithstanding the appearance of service) have been undeserving their regard or that they are remiss towards me. Their silence is to me something like condemnation, and their neglect must be justified by my loss of reputation, or my reputation supported at their injury; either of which is alike painful to me. But as I have ever been dumb on everything which might touch national honor, so I mean ever to continue so."

The visit took place, and on November 5th Washington and Paine celebrated the Gunpowder Plot by setting the river alight. The gas, freed by the poles of the soldiers, rose to the surface of the water and was ignited by Washington with cartridge paper—an effective and economical entertainment. The visit was, however, productive of something better than gas bubbles. Washington tried to persuade Congress to make some financial recognition of Paine's services. Unfortunately, Paine's insistence on the supremacy of the central government had earned him the dislike of certain members of Congress, and when their hostility became apparent it was decided that the matter should be left to the individual states.

Early in 1784 New York voted Paine a house and farm of 277 acres at New Rochelle. He went to take possession of it, celebrating the occasion with a village fête. He was known to the villagers by the name of his most famous pamphlet, and the children, believing it to be his real name, addressed him as "Mr. Common Sense." One little girl was much impressed by his kindness to everybody and many years afterwards remembered how he had "sat in the shade and assisted in the labor of the feast by cutting or breaking sugar to be used in some agreeable liquids by his guests." He did not remain at New Rochelle, but returned to his friends at Bordentown, where he burst into poetry, writing four patriotic songs.

Washington sent letters to friends in Virginia and Pennsylvania urging them to use what influence they had to obtain grants for Paine. "If you view his services in the American cause in the same important light that I do, I am sure you will have pleasure in obtaining it for him," he wrote to R. H. Lee, and to James Madison: "Can nothing be done in our Assembly for poor Paine? Must the merits and services of *Common Sense* continue to glide down the stream of time, unrewarded by this country?" Washington even made it known that if the states did not make the necessary provision, he would do so himself.

The Virginia Legislature considered the gift of a piece of land to Paine, but they had not forgotten that he had "written a pamphlet injurious to our claim of Western Territory," and while willing to pay for a statue to Washington, they would not present a farm to Paine. The Pennsylvania Assembly, on the other hand, voted him £500; and Congress, stung into action at last, made him a payment of $3,000, which did not even cover the expenses of his journey to France, when he had saved the nation and returned home penniless.

Paine never grasped the simple truth that people do not value what they receive for nothing; moreover, they dislike being reminded of virtues lacking in themselves. Throughout his life Paine remained inexorably generous and implacably benevolent, and naturally he provoked the keenest resentment wherever he went.

Congress sat in New York during 1785, and Paine, the leading literary figure of the time, took part in the social life of the place, often visiting the house of Commodore Nicholson, the main haunt of leading republicans. In Philadelphia that year an "exhibition of patriotic paintings" included a portrait of Paine, who by the name of "Common Sense" was as well known to the man-in-the-street as George Washington. He was on a very friendly footing with Franklin, just returned from Europe, and together they made innumerable experiments. When apart they wrote to one another at great length on tallow candles, paper money, steam-engines, iron bridges, and what not; and when together their discussions on such topics lasted far into the night. Franklin called Paine his "adopted political son." Paine called Franklin "my patron" and could finish a long letter to him in this manner: "I do not, my dear Sir, offer these reasons to you but to myself, for I have often observed that by lending words for my thoughts I understand my thoughts the better. Thoughts are a kind of mental smoke, which require words to illuminate them."

The subjects which chiefly occupied the mind and pen of Paine from 1785 to 1787 were finance and bridge-building. There was a movement to repeal the charter granted to the Bank of North America, which had been started by the subscription he had set on foot for the relief of the army. The movement was in the interests of paper money and Paine wrote a "dissertation" on the subject which had the effect of maintaining the charter. His action gained him the formidable animosity of certain large financial interests, and his friends were concerned for his personal safety, fearing, whenever he failed to keep an appointment, that he had been the victim of foul play. Paine himself did not suffer from nerves and was soon absorbed in the problem of constructing a bridge with a single span, which he hoped the authorities would approve for erection over the Schuylkill and other rivers where "a bridge on piers will never answer." He made three models, the first of wood, the second of cast iron, the third of wrought iron, each consisting of one arch, because "the European method of bridge architecture, by piers and arches, is not adapted to many of the rivers in America on account of the ice in the winter." His bridges would leave "the whole passage of the river clear of the incumbrance of piers," whereas the ordinary method of bridge-construction, advocated by the Agricultural Society, would be worse than useless: "They may sink money, but they never will sink piers that will stand."

A committee was appointed by the Pennsylvania Assembly to report on Paine's bridge. But while it was still sitting and reporting he decided to visit Europe. His father, now seventy-eight, had recently written him an affectionate letter and he was anxious to see his parents again. Furthermore, it was beginning to dawn upon him that he would have a much better chance of getting his bridge accepted in America if he could obtain for it the approval of French engineers. With letters of introduction from Franklin to Vergennes and other Frenchmen of note—"for it so often happens," he said, "that men live to forfeit the reputation at one time they gained at another, that it is prudent not to presume too much on one's self"—he sailed for Europe in April, 1787.

Thomas Paine was now fifty years of age, and for one of his achievement it might have been expected that he could look forward to a serene old age, spent in the country he had fought for, among a people he more than anyone had helped to set free; for the pen of Paine was mightier than the sword of Washington. His fate was ordered otherwise. He went to Europe for a few months; he stayed there for fifteen years; and in that time he managed to make a world-wide reputation and to become the object of universal execration. It would be as well to pause at this point and take stock of a character that was to suffer so many vicissitudes, to see as clearly as we can the man who, having caused a revolution in the New World, was about to set the Old World by the ears, and finally to bring a hornets' nest from both worlds about his own ears. He is well worth looking at, because no one in history ever stirred up so much strife, aroused so much enmity, or so violently affected the thoughts and actions of human beings.

Perhaps it is unnecessary to say that he was a man of peace, charity, gentleness and sweet reasonableness, whose motto was "The world is my country, and my religion is to do good." He once wrote to Washington: "You will observe, sir, that my reasoning is founded on the supposition of their being reasonable beings, which if they are not, then they are not within the compass of my system." And his advice on how to handle a political party ran: "Next to the gaining a majority is that of keeping it. This, at least in my opinion, will not be best accomplished by doing or attempting a great deal of business, but by doing no more than is absolutely necessary to be done, acting moderately and giving no offence." In social life, too, he favored compromise and logic: "Never give a deciding opinion between two persons you are in friendship with, lest you lose one by it; whilst doing so between two persons, your supposed enemies, may make one your friend."

But though a man of much sagacity in his writings, sound sense in his advice, and diplomacy in his general dealings, he was at the mercy of his temperament when his judgment was called in question. Transparently honest and unaffectedly simple by nature, he had the defects of those qualities: he was assertive and dogmatic, impetuous and unimaginative. Praise went to his head and he developed a strong sense of his own importance. He constantly referred, with justifiable pride, to the wonderful work he had done, knew most of his pamphlets by heart, and frequently quoted from them. Gérard said that he was "puffed up by the success of his political writings." This incapacitated him from appreciating points of view opposed to his own and gave a tincture of pharisaism to his moral and political attitude. If people disagreed with him, they were wrong. Conscious of personal integrity, he was so sure that what he said was true that he failed to see how any honest person could pursue a different line of thought. Therefore disagreement with him argued dishonesty in his opponent. Personal ambition, personal greed, disgusted him, and he was quite unable to perceive that his love of fame, his *im*personal ambition, was merely another manifestation of that inner force which impelled his spiritual inferiors to less noble forms of self-expression. This made him intolerant of human weaknesses he did not share, and thus there was a certain narrowness in his honesty which aroused the bitterest animosity in equally assertive but more fallible human beings.

Convinced of his rectitude he could not brook contradiction, and though he put the highest value on reason he became unreasonable when anyone reasoned with him. "I swear to God it was so!" exclaimed a man he had accused of error. "I swear to God it was *not* so!" shouted Paine, and the man felt he had been ill-used. "That, by God, is a lie!" was how he once broke into a financial discussion, which naturally developed into a quarrel ending in "very high words." While holding forth on any subject he could not bear interruption; even inattention annoyed him; and once the fall of a poker in the grate irritated him so much that he stopped talking abruptly and nothing could induce him to proceed.

As a rule, though, while easily provoked, he was quickly appeased by signs of contrition, and no one could be more delightful in company when he was in the mood. Symptoms of uncommon intelligence in a gathering had an exhilarating effect upon him and, once started, he would draw on an inexhaustible fund of anecdote which, if appreciated, had the effect of exciting him, like an actor who is intoxicated with applause and strives to bring down the house. But he was a creature of extremes, subject to very low and very high spirits, and it often happened that he was taciturn in the presence of more than two or three people. A "Society for Political Inquiries" used to meet in Franklin's library, and it is recorded that Paine never opened his mouth. Most of his friends asserted that he was reserved and thoughtful in company, seldom mingling in the common chit-chat of dinner table or social assembly.

In appearance he was of good middle height, five feet nine or ten inches, broad-shouldered and of spare, athletic build. His face was oblong in shape, its normal expression solemn and reflective unless lit up by the effect of his own conversation. His nose was prominent. His eyes were remarkably full, brilliant, and lively, and so piercing in quality that they gave the impression of being black. General Charles Lee said that he had "genius in his eyes." They were certainly his most noticeable feature. His carriage was upright, but he stood and walked without stiffness or affectation. His legs and feet were described by a lady as "elegant." In fact, he appears to have been what is called "a well-made man." His dress was clean though careless; he wore his hair queued with side-curls and powdered, after the fashion of French gentlemen; he carried neither sword nor cane; when out walking he usually held his hat in one hand, placing the other behind his back. His manners were easy and gracious; his conversation was frank and natural, grave with strangers, playful among friends. He disliked profanity and indecent stories, good-humoredly rebuking such friends as indulged in them. When praised or greeted with affection his sober countenance relaxed and a "benignant smile" irradiated his features. He never used the common greeting, "How d'ye do?" but always asked, "What news?" He was touchy in all matters concerning his personal life and opinions, not caring to be questioned too closely about them, and once even described as impertinent the simple query, "What do you think of that?"

When not irritated by contradiction or ruffled by opposition, his thoughts and actions were careful and orderly. Even his anecdotes were always told in the same words and broken up with the same pauses. He did not like poetry because it was not rational, which is much the same as not liking apple dumpling because it is not rice pudding. He was fond of children and developed a habit of keeping sweets for them in his pocket. He was also fond of animals, which he patted and talked to; but unlike most child-and-animal lovers, he was equally fond of grown-up people. His personal indulgences were few: he took a fair amount of snuff, drank a certain amount of brandy and rum, and, being naturally indolent, rose late in the mornings. Not a born worker, he often found it difficult to begin the day's toil, but when once engaged he seemed to delight in difficulties, especially when dealing with mechanical problems.

Such was the man who now stood on the threshold of world-wide fame, and was so soon to enter the portal of world-wide infamy. Benjamin Franklin once said to him: "Where liberty is, there is my country." Thomas Paine replied: "Where liberty is not, there is mine." And since he always acknowledged himself a citizen of the world, the time was bound to come when no country in the world would acknowledge him as its citizen.

## Chapter VI

### RETURN OF THE REBEL

ARRIVED in Paris, he was soon in touch with Thomas Jefferson, who had succeeded Franklin as American minister, and Lafayette, with whom he had been intimate during the War of Independence. The letters of introduction from Franklin were quite unnecessary because his fame had preceded him. He was received with honor by the Academy of Sciences, which at once chose a committee to deal with his bridge. The committee were unprepared for "such an unprecedented thing" as an arch of four or five hundred feet; and since it was their custom to give reasons for their opinions, they took some time over the report. What chiefly embarrassed them was the difficulty of explaining how a bridge constructed on such principles could be so strong. Eventually they approved Paine's model as simpler, stronger, and lighter than any model that had been submitted to them by a Frenchman.

During this visit Paine got to know several people of interest, including Danton, Cordorcet, and the chief Minister, Cardinal Loménie de Brienne, Archbishop of Toulouse, of whose appointment as Controller of Finances Carlyle wrote: "Unhappy only that it took such talent and industry to *gain* the place; that to *qualify* for it hardly any talent or industry was left disposable." The Cardinal was a man of advanced ideas and Paine was delighted to find that he was not only against "the madness of war," but actually favored "a better understanding with England." A year or so later Paine's good opinion of him seemed more than ever justified, for Brienne invited a number of "thinkers" to discuss the affairs of the nation and to find a way out of its financial difficulties, or, as Carlyle put it: "Invitation to Chaos to be so kind as build, out of its tumultuous driftwood, an Ark of Escape for him!"

Having dispatched his bridge model to Sir Joseph Banks, president of the Royal Society, Paine followed it to London early in September, 1787. He took lodgings in York Street, St. James's, saw Banks about the bridge, saw Burke about Brienne's desire to reach an understanding with England, and then went on to Thetford. His father had died the previous November, though the news had not reached him before his arrival in France, but his mother was healthy at ninety and living in comparative comfort on the money he had been able to send her from time to time. He now made her a regular allowance of nine shillings a week, which probably supplied all her needs, for she lived to the age of ninety-four. With occasional journeys to London and elsewhere in connection with his bridge, he stayed at Thetford long enough for his mother to revise her early estimation of him as "an undutiful son." He spent the days in writing and meditation and revisiting old haunts and reflecting on things past and musing on things to come, and wondering how it was that, while everything had altered, nothing seemed changed. He tramped the lanes, sat in the Quaker meeting-house, wrote long letters to Jefferson, corrected a pamphlet he had written against war, with special reference to Pitt's designs against Holland, deeply considered the individual rights of man in society, and jotted down innumerable notes as ideas for inventions and improvements flashed across his brain at odd moments—a planing-machine, a novel form of crane, a smokeless candle, a new kind of wheel, the use of gunpowder to provide motion, and so on.

Most of his energy in 1788 was devoted to his bridge. Patents for England, Scotland, and Ireland were granted in September, and Messrs. Walker of Rotherham in Yorkshire undertook the construction. He wished to exhibit it in London, afterwards putting it up for sale, and both profits and expenses were to be divided equally between himself and the Walkers. He spent much time at Rotherham, was quickly on visiting

terms with the workmen and their families, and was so
much liked that the tradition of his kindness and benevolence lingered in that district till the children of those
who had known him were gathered to their fathers. Sir
Joseph Banks was enthusiastic about his model, referring to "those emanations of spirit which taught you
to construct a bridge without any reference to the means
used by your predecessors in that art."

At last it was ready, and an American merchant in
London, Peter Whiteside, thinking there was something
to be made out of it, helped Paine with the expenses of
its transport by water from Yorkshire and its erection
on Paddington Green, London, in June, 1790. Many
people paid their shilling to see it, and all might have
gone well if Whiteside had not suddenly become a
bankrupt. With great difficulty Paine raised the sum of
£620, which was debited to the bridge in Whiteside's
books, and it is probable that even after this loss the invention would have brought him in a small fortune but
for the fact that the French Revolution had broken out
and diverted his attention from the bridge to Edmund
Burke. After he had left England for good the material of his invention was used for the arched bridge of
236 feet span across the river Wear at Sunderland,
which was finished in 1796.

But we must go back a little. Rather to his surprise
the leading Whigs had taken him up when he arrived
in England. The Duke of Portland, the Marquis of

Lansdowne, Burke, and Fox, seemed anxious to consult him and to pay him respect. They were of course desirous, on returning to power, to make commercial agreements with America; and knowing that Paine was in the confidence of Washington, Jefferson, and Franklin, they thought that by making much of him he would make much of them and so prepare a friendly atmosphere for future negotiation. He stayed at the country seats of Burke and the Duke of Portland. He dined often with Lord Fitzwilliam at Wentworth House. Peers were polite to him, duchesses were deferential. His opinions were heard with close attention; his bridge was inspected with studious care; he was flattered, caressed, welcomed with ceremony, with effusion, patted on the shoulder, called "my esteemed friend."

It was all very pleasant, and at first Mr. Paine seemed duly impressed, but their compliments were wasted because he had a much higher opinion of himself than they could conceive possible. As politicians he held them in contempt: "All the great services that are done in the world are performed by volunteer characters, who accept nothing for them," he would say; "but the routine of office is always regulated to such a general standard of abilities as to be within the compass of numbers in every country to perform, and therefore cannot merit very extraordinary recompense. 'Government,' says Swift, 'is a plain thing, and fitted to the capacity of many heads.'" What value was their patronage to a Paine? What achievement could they claim in comparison with his? "With all the inconvenience of early life against me, I am proud to say that with a perseverance undismayed by difficulties, a disinterestedness that compelled respect, I have not only contributed to raise a new empire in the world, founded on a new system of government, but I have arrived at an eminence in political literature, the most difficult of all lines to succeed and excel in, which Aristocracy with all its aids has not been able to reach or to rival." Proud words, which were not a mask to cover a feeling of inferiority. He meant them. That was how he really felt about it.

As time went on it began to dawn upon his hosts that he was not exactly eating out of their hands. It almost seemed as if their attentions to him were received as a right; and when the novelty of treating him as an equal wore off, they began to resent being treated by him as an equal. They had at last stumbled across an answer to Shakespeare's question, "For who so firm that cannot be seduced?" The answer was "Tom Paine," and it did not please them. "I believe I am not so much in the good graces of the Marquis of Lansdowne as I used to be—I do not answer his purpose," wrote Paine to Jefferson: "He was always talking of a sort of reconnection of England and America, and my coldness and reserve on this subject checked communication." No doubt the Marquis thought that there was not much advantage in being a nobleman when one was treated by an ex-staymaker with coldness and reserve. Paine annoyed these politicians, too, because he did not adapt his views to his surroundings. As Whigs they were all for progress, but they drew the line at democracy. It was difficult to know what to say when an honored guest at one's own table came out with remarks like:

"A gentleman of large property may hunt on the ground of a man of small property; while the man of small property may not hunt on his own ground."

After all, the leading Whigs themselves were property-holders; and they could not be expected, even as progressives, to appreciate the full flavor of this:

"It is the same crime to murder the king or to plunge the country in a civil war, as to coin a sixpence. To plunge the country in an unnecessary foreign war is no crime whatever."

Or this:

"The poor man is hanged for taking a loaf from the baker's shop to satisfy the cravings of nature; the baker who cheats a whole parish is fined a few shillings; and the great man who plunders the nation of thousands goes unpunished."

Let alone this:

"There is no body of men more jealous of their privileges than the Commons—because they sell them."

And they definitely drew the line at this:

"A man is said to be as drunk as an owl when he cannot see, as drunk as a sow when he wallows in the dirt, as drunk as a beggar when he is impudent, as drunk as the devil when he is inclined to mischief, and as drunk as a lord when he is everything that is bad."

Was this merely a sign of low breeding? No, it was just damned impertinence, for which the fellow ought to be soundly whipped in the pillory.

However, he was an important person in America, and America meant money; so they bottled down their wrath, smiled a little wryly, comforted themselves with the reflection that he had once been a gauger and would probably end on the gallows, and slowly, diplomatically, dropped him.

Not only the respectable tradesman class, but such hangers-on to the nobility as Benjamin West, who succeeded Reynolds as president of the Royal Academy, felt a little uncomfortable in the company of a man who was liable to slip remarks of this kind into the general conversation:

"The law is equally open to the poor and the rich: so is the London Tavern"—or, as we might say, so is the Ritz Hotel.

"To wound cattle is a capital crime, to wound a man only a misdemeanour."

"If by my industry I make my land ten times its former value, I must pay ten times as much to the priest."

On the announcement of the news that Mr. Dundas

had just received the freedom of a certain Scottish burgh in a little gold box, Paine observed, "Their freedom might be contained in a very little box indeed."

"If I were obliged to accept a title," he informed a large company, "it would be that of knighthood, as the infamy of it would not descend on my family."

He was always a trifle intractable on the subject of hereditary distinctions:

"A man must serve a seven-years apprenticeship to a shoemaker, but all our peers and a great proportion of our commoners are born legislators. Nor is this all; if the shoemaker, after all his study, do not make shoes to please his customers, they will not employ him; but we are obliged to receive all the manufactures of the other profession I have mentioned, be they good or bad."

Some one having quoted John Selden's "Ignorance of the law excuses no man," Paine nodded. "Every man is bound to know all the laws," he agreed, adding, after a pause, "although it will take fifteen guineas to purchase them and a professional education to understand them." The laws were made to keep the mighty in their seats and to depress the humble and meek: "If a man is tried at the quarter sessions for a petty assault, it will cost him more if he is acquitted than if he shall be convicted," he said.

We get a snapshot of him at this period in the lodgings of a friend. John Wolcot, who wrote satires and lampoons over the name of "Peter Pindar," was present. Paine was dressed "in a snuff-coloured coat, olive velvet vest, drab breeches, coarse hose" and wore "shoe buckles of the size of a half dollar." He maintained that the minority in all deliberative bodies ought in all cases to govern the majority. Wolcot smiled. "You must grant me," pursued Paine, "that the proportion of men of sense to the ignorant among mankind is at least twenty, thirty, or even forty-nine, to an hundred. The majority of mankind are consequently most prone to error; and if we achieve the right, the minority ought in all cases to govern." Wolcot remained unconvinced; so the question was put to the vote and all agreed with Paine except Wolcot, who then remarked: "I am the wise minority who ought in all cases to govern your ignorant majority."

Up to the beginning of 1789 Paine was still in a position to report to Jefferson: "I am in some intimacy with Mr. Burke, and after the new ministry are formed he has proposed to introduce me to them." But as that year wore on the dropping process already alluded to became marked and he envied Jefferson, who was about to leave Paris for home: "Absent from America I feel a craving desire to return," he wrote, "and I can scarcely forbear weeping at the thoughts of your going and my staying behind. . . . Remember me with an overflowing affection to my dear America—the people and the place. Be so kind to shake hands with them for

me, and tell our beloved General Washington and my
old friend Dr. Franklin how much I long to see them."

All through the year 1789 his mind was much occupied with America and he felt stifled by the atmosphere
of aimlessness, reaction, stagnation and frustration that
surrounded him in England. He tried to shake off the
feeling of oppression that too often crept over him, by
journeying from place to place to see the factories which
were beginning to blacken the English countryside but
which heralded for him the dawn of a new world, an
enlightened world, a world of science and progress and
beauty and the brotherhood of man. He visited the cot-
ton mills in Lancashire, the potteries in Staffordshire;
he saw steel furnaces and was shown the mysteries of
tin-plate and white-lead manufacture; and he thought
how easy it would be to introduce all these things into
America and make that land flow with milk and honey,
or at least silk and money.

His heart was at home in the country where his mind
was not cramped. "The natural mightiness of America
expands the mind, and it partakes of the greatness it
contemplates," he once wrote, and never did he express
his emotions so fully as in a letter he sent this year to
Kitty, the daughter of his friend, Commodore Nicholson. He had known the Nicholson girls from their
school days at Bordentown and had seen much of them
later in New York. They were very fond of him, and
he of them, and the news that Kitty was about to be

married to Colonel Few drew a letter from him which touched a note we do not hear again in his correspondence:

"I very affectionately congratulate Mr. and Mrs. Few on their happy marriage, and every branch of the families allied by that connection; and I request my fair correspondent to present me to her partner, and to say, for me, that he has obtained one of the highest Prizes on the wheel. Besides the pleasure which your letter gives me to hear you are all happy and well, it relieves me from a sensation not easy to be dismissed; and if you will excuse a few full thoughts for obtruding themselves into a congratulatory letter, I will tell you what it is. When I see my female friends drop off by matrimony I am sensible of something that affects me like a loss in spite of all the appearances of joy: I cannot help mixing the sincere compliment of regret with that of congratulation. It appears as if I had outlived or lost a friend. It seems to me as if the original was no more, and that which she is changed to forsakes the circle and forgets the scenes of former society. Felicities and cares superior to those she formerly cared for, create to her a new landscape of Life that excludes the little friendships of the past. It is not every lady's mind that is sufficiently capacious to prevent those greater objects crowding out the less, or that can spare a thought to former friendships after she has given her hand and heart to the man who loves her. But the sentiment your letter contains has prevented these dull Ideas from mixing with the congratulation I present you, and is so congenial with the enlarged opinion I have always formed of you, that at the time I read your letter with pleasure. I read it with pride, because it convinces me that I have some judgment in that most difficult science —a Lady's mind. Most sincerely do I wish you all the good that Heaven can bless you with, and as you have in your own family an example of domestic happiness you are already in the knowledge of obtaining it. That no condition we can enjoy is an exemption from care— that some shade will mingle itself with the brightest sunshine of Life—that even our affections may become the instruments of our sorrows—that the sweet felicities of home depend on good temper as well as on good sense, and that there is always something to forgive even in the nearest and dearest of our friends,—are truths which, tho' too obvious to be told, ought never to be forgotten; and I know you will not esteem my friendship the less for impressing them upon you.

"Though I appear a sort of wanderer, the married state has not a sincerer friend than I am. It is the harbour of human life, and is, with respect to the things of this world, what the next world is to this. It is home; and that one word conveys more than any other word can express. For a few years we may glide along the tide of youthful single life and be wonderfully delighted; but it is a tide that flows but once, and what is still worse, it ebbs faster than it flows, and leaves many a hapless voyager aground. I am one, you see, that have experienced the fate I am describing. I have lost my tide;[1] it passed by while every thought of my heart was on the wing for the salvation of my dear America, and I have now, as contentedly as I can, made myself a little bower of willows on the shore that has the solitary resemblance of a home. Should I always continue the tenant of this home, I hope my female acquaintance will ever remember that it contains not the churlish enemy of their sex, not the inaccessible cold-hearted mortal, nor the capricious-tempered oddity, but one of the best and most affectionate of their friends.

"I did not forget the Dunstable hat, but it was not on wear here when I arrived. That I am a negligent correspondent I freely confess, and I always reproach myself for it. . . .

"I thank you for the details of news you give. Kiss Molly Field for me and wish her joy,—and all the good girls of Bordentown. How is my favorite Sally Morris, my boy Joe, and my horse Button? pray let me know. Polly and Nancy Rogers,—are they married? or do they intend to build bowers as I have done? If they do, I wish they would twist their green willows somewhere near to mine. . . .

"You touch me on a very tender part when you say

[1] Paine had never mentioned his early marital affairs in America, partly because he wanted to forget them, partly because his enemies would have used them to discredit his writings, and partly, no doubt, because, had he wanted to marry again, they might have stood in his way.

my friends on your side the water 'cannot be reconciled to the idea of my resigning my adopted America, even for my native England.' They are right. Though I am in as elegant style of acquaintance here as any American that ever came over, my heart and myself are 3,000 miles apart; and I had rather see my horse Button in his own stable, or eating the grass of Bordentown or Morrisania, than see all the pomp and show of Europe.

"A thousand years hence (for I must indulge in a few thoughts), perhaps in less, America may be what England now is! The innocence of her character that won the hearts of all nations in her favor may sound like a romance, and her inimitable virtue as if it had never been. The ruins of that liberty which thousands bled for, or suffered to obtain, may just furnish materials for a village tale or extort a sigh from rustic sensibility, while the fashionable of that day, enveloped in dissipation, shall deride the principle and deny the fact.

"When we contemplate the fall of Empires and the extinction of nations of the ancient world, we see but little to excite our regret than the mouldering ruins of pompous palaces, magnificent monuments, lofty pyramids, and walls and towers of the most costly workmanship. But when the Empire of America shall fall, the subject for contemplative sorrow will be infinitely greater than crumbling brass or marble can inspire. It will not then be said, here stood a temple of vast antiquity,—here rose a Babel of invisible height, or there a palace of sumptuous extravagance; but here, ah painful thought! the noblest work of human wisdom, the grandest scene of human glory, the fair cause of freedom rose and fell!

"Read this and then ask if I forget America.—But I'll not be dull if I can help it, so I leave off, and close my letter tomorrow, which is the day the mail is made up for America.

(*Next day*.) "I have heard this morning with extreme concern of the death of our worthy friend Capt. Read. Mrs. Read lives in a house of mine at Bordentown, and you will much oblige me by telling her how much I am affected by her loss; and to mention to her, with that delicacy which such an offer and her situation require, and which no one knows better how to convey than yourself, that the two years' rent which is due I request her to accept of, and to consider herself at home till she hears further from me. . . .

"I am always distressed at closing a letter, because it seems like taking leave of my friends after a parting conversation.—Captain Nicholson, Mrs. Nicholson, Hannah, Fanny, James, and the little ones, and you my dear Kitty, and your partner for life—God bless you all! and send me safe back to my much loved America!

THOMAS PAINE—aet. 52.

or if you better like it

'Common Sense'.

"This comes by the packet which sails from Falmouth, 300 miles from London; but by the first vessel from London to New York I will send you some magazines. In the meantime be so kind as to write to me by the first opportunity. Remember me to the family at Morrisania, and all my friends at New York and Bordentown. Desire Gen. Morris to take another guinea of Mr. Constable, who has some money of mine in his hands, and give it to my boy Joe. Tell Sally to take care of 'Button' . . ."

---

## Chapter VII

## THE RIGHTS OF MAN

---

ON JULY 14, 1789, the Bastille fell, and in the autumn of that year Paine, ever fervent in the cause of freedom, was in Paris. Jefferson had left, and Paine, whose authorship of *Common Sense* had gained him a considerable reputation in France, was looked upon by Lafayette, as the representative of America. Lafayette, therefore, gave him the key of the Bastille to present to General Washington as a symbol of the fact that "the principles of America" had caused the fall of "that detestable prison." In forwarding the key to Washington in May, 1790, Paine revealed his simplicity of mind in the suggestion that the General should write to congratulate the king and queen of France "on the happy example they are giving to Europe." He sent Washington the political news of the moment, expressed his sorrow at being unable to make the presentation in person, "but I doubt I shall not be able to see my much-loved America till next Spring," announced that he would carry the American flag in the procession when the French Constitution was proclaimed, and inclosed half a dozen razors made at the works where his bridge was being constructed "as a little token from a very grateful heart."

His presence in Paris at the festivities in connection with the new Constitution was recorded by Carlyle in this manner: "Nor is our England without her missionaries. She has . . . her Paine: rebellious Staymaker; unkempt; who feels that he, a single Needleman, did, by his *Common Sense* pamphlet, free America;—that he can and will free all this world; perhaps even the other."

Early in November, 1790, Edmund Burke's *Reflections* on the French Revolution was published. Paine was staying just then at the Angel inn, Islington, and immediately began to write his reflections on Burke. His thoughts expanded, went beyond Burke and embraced mankind. The book, which was continued in Harding Street, Fetter Lane, and completed in Versailles, came out as *The Rights of Man.*

For a century and a quarter after his death the fame of Edmund Burke as a political thinker and an honest man increased with every book that was written about him. A good deal of his reputation for honesty may have been due to Johnson's favorable opinion of him. But even those who are not intelligent enough to per-

ceive that the trade of politics has always attracted the
vainest and most self-seeking members of the community have at last begun to see through Burke, whose
reputation is now on the wane. His "profound truths"
have become superficial platitudes; his "honesty," in
the matter of Warren Hastings, for example, has
proved to be self-interest. Paine, though he was taken
in by Burke's apparently disinterested attitude towards
the American Revolution, did not need so many weeks
as posterity has required years to find him out. But
then Paine had the advantage of knowing him personally; he had seen him drunk and seen him sober, and
knew that he was less dangerous under the influence of
alcohol than under the influence of a pension. At a first
glance Burke's book on the French Revolution contained more signs of an unstable intellect than any work
ever written by a man with a reputation for genius. But
at a close inspection it was found to contain signs, not of
mental derangement, but of a monetary arrangement.
He had been, Paine discovered, "a masked pensioner
at £1,500 per annum for about ten years," and he had
hopes, which eventually fructified, of a still larger pension. Thirty thousand copies of his book were circulated
in the courts and among the aristocracy of Europe, and
he privately advised Marie Antoinette to trust in the
support of foreign artists to enslave the French people.

Paine, of course, had no difficulty in demolishing
Burke. A man who could seriously suggest that a parlia-

mentary declaration, made to William and Mary a century before, was binding *forever* on the people of England,[1] and that as a consequence the English people
would never be able to choose their own government;
such a man could only be treated as a joke, and Paine
proceeded to pull his leg: "The Parliament of 1688
might as well have passed an act to have authorized
themselves to live for ever, as to make their authority
live for ever." Apparently Burke's book was written
with the object of instructing the French nation: "It is
darkness attempting to illuminate light," commented
Paine, who described Burke's periods as finishing "with
music in the ear and nothing in the heart," summed up
his book as a "tribute of fear," and dealt with it from
this angle:

"I know a place in America called Point-no-Point,
because as you proceed along the shore, gay and flowery
as Mr. Burke's language, it continually recedes and pre-
sents itself as a distance before you; but when you have
got as far as you can go, there is no point at all. Just
thus it is with Mr. Burke's three hundred and fifty-six
pages. It is therefore difficult to reply to him. But as the
points he wishes to establish may be inferred from what
he abuses, it is in his paradoxes that we must look for
his arguments."

Burke had wept tears of distress over the plight of

---

[1] "The Lords Spiritual and Temporal, and Commons, do, in the name
of the people aforesaid, most humbly and faithfully submit themselves,
their heirs and posterities for ever."

the king and queen, but did not give a thought to the millions who had suffered poverty or imprisonment: "Nature has been kinder to Mr. Burke than he is to her. He is not affected by the reality of distress touching his heart, but by the showy resemblance of it striking his imagination. He pities the plumage, but forgets the dying bird. . . . His hero or his heroine must be a tragedy-victim expiring in show, and not the real prisoner of misery, sliding into death in the silence of a dungeon."

Naturally Burke had made the most of the occasional excesses of mob violence which had followed the outbreak. Paine effectively countered the accusation: "When men are sore with the sense of oppressions, and menaced with the prospect of new ones, is the calmness of philosophy or the palsy of insensibility to be looked for?" Brutality of this kind was learned by the people from the governments they lived under. Teach governments humanity and the people would soon learn the lesson. The barbarity of governments taught people to be barbarous: "It is by distortedly exalting some men, that others are distortedly debased, till the whole is out of nature. A vast mass of mankind are degradedly thrown into the background of the human picture, to bring forward, with greater glare, the puppet-show of State and Aristocracy. In the commencement of a Revolution, those men are rather the followers of the *camp* than of the *standard* of Liberty, and have yet to be instructed how to reverence it."

Paine described the circumstances which led to the taking of the Bastille and the incidents which followed its fall. Dealing quickly and easily with Burke's "precedents" and appeals to the past, he then put the whole case for the natural rights of man which dated from the creation of the first man: "Natural rights are those which appertain to man in right of his existence. Of this kind are all the intellectual rights, or rights of the mind, and also all those rights of acting as an individual for his own comfort and happiness, which are not injurious to the natural rights of others. Civil rights are those which appertain to man in right of his being a member of society. Every civil right has for its foundation some natural right pre-existing in the individual, but to the enjoyment of which his individual power is not, in all cases, sufficiently competent. Of this kind are all those which relate to security and protection."

But governments which denied man his rights had come into being. How? By superstition (priestcraft) and power (conquerors). These two, Church and State, had eventually joined hands for mutual support: "The key of St. Peter and the key of the Treasury became quartered on one another, and the wondering cheated multitude worshipped the invention." He traced the history of governments, noting that England was without a constitution, like the genius of Burke: "It is a genius at random, and not a genius constituted. But he must say something. He has therefore mounted in the air like a balloon, to draw the eyes of the multitude from the ground they stand upon." The English Parliament was "like a man being both mortgager and mortgagee, and in the case of misapplication of trust it is the criminal sitting in judgment upon himself. If those who vote the supplies are the same persons who receive the supplies when voted, and are to account for the expenditure of those supplies to those who voted them, it is *themselves accountable to themselves*, and the Comedy of Errors concludes with the Pantomime of Hush. . . . They order these things better in France."

For example, the French Constitution said that "the right of war and peace is in the nation. Where else should it reside but in those who are to pay the expence? In England this right is said to reside in a *metaphor* shown at the Tower for sixpence or a shilling apiece." But in England it did not matter whether the right resided in the Crown or Parliament: "War is the common harvest of all those who participate in the division and expenditure of public money, in all countries. It is the art of *conquering at home*; the object of it is an increase of revenue; and as revenue cannot be increased without taxes, a pretence must be made for expenditures. In reviewing the history of the English Government, its wars and its taxes, a bystander, not blinded by prejudice nor warped by interest, would declare that taxes were not raised to carry on wars, but that wars were raised to carry on taxes."

There was another anachronism that ought to be swept away: "The French Constitution says, *There shall be no titles;* and, of consequence, all that class of equivocal generation which in some countries is called *aristocracy* and in others *nobility*, is done away, and the *peer* is exalted into MAN. Titles are but nicknames, and every nickname is a title. The thing is perfectly harmless in itself, but it marks a sort of foppery in the human character, which degrades it. It reduces man into the diminutive of man in things which are great, and the counterfeit of woman in things which are little. It talks about its fine *blue ribbon* like a girl, and shows its new *garter* like a child. A certain writer, of some antiquity, says: 'When I was a child, I thought as a child; but when I became a man, I put away childish things.' It is, properly, from the elevated mind of France that the folly of titles has fallen. It has outgrown the baby cloaths of *Count* and *Duke*, and breeched itself in manhood. France has not leveled, it has exalted. It has put down the dwarf, to set up the man. The punyism of a senseless word like *Duke* or *Count* or *Earl* has ceased to please. Even those who possessed them have disowned the gibberish, and as they outgrew the rickets, have despised the rattle. The genuine mind of man, thirsting for its native home, society, contemns the gewgaws that separate him from it. Titles are like circles drawn by the magician's wand, to contract the sphere of man's felicity. He lives immured within the Bastille of a word, and surveys at a distance the envied life of man." As for allowing titles to rule citizens, "the idea of hereditary legislators is as inconsistent as that of hereditary judges, or hereditary juries; and as absurd as an hereditary mathematician, or an hereditary wise man; and as ridiculous as an hereditary poet-laureate."

In describing the alterations that had already taken place in France and those that ought to have taken place in England, Paine made several remarks that are as true today, and therefore as irritating, as when he made them:

"The difference between a republican and a courtier with respect to monarchy, is that the one opposes monarchy, believing it to be something; and the other laughs at it, knowing it to be nothing."

The French National Assembly "are not in the case of a ministerial or opposition party in England, who, though they are opposed, are still united to keep up the common mystery."

"Aristocracy is a kind of fungus growing out of the corruption of society."

"The Nobility, or rather No-ability."

"It is easy to conceive that a band of interested men, such as placement, pensioners, lords of the bedchamber, lords of the kitchen, lords of the necessary-house, and the Lord knows what besides, can find as many reasons for Monarchy as their salaries, paid at the expence of the country, amount to."

"As war is the system of Government on the old construction, the animosity which Nations reciprocally entertain is nothing more than what the policy of their Governments excites to keep up the spirit of the system. Each Government accuses the other of perfidy, intrigue, and ambition, as a means of heating the imagination of their respective Nations, and incensing them to hostilities. Man is not the enemy of Man, but through the medium of a false system of Government. Instead, therefore, of exclaiming against the ambition of Kings, the exclamation should be directed against the principle of such Governments; and instead of seeking to reform the individual, the wisdom of a Nation should apply itself to reform the system."

None of these remarks endeared Paine to the ruling classes; but the success of his book was without precedent in England, as *Common Sense* had been in America. Over fifty thousand copies were sold in a few weeks, and as usual the author refused to benefit from it, giving the proceeds to the Society for Constitutional Information, while he himself was occupying what a visitor called "wretched apartments" both in London and in Paris. For a time he was one of the most popular men in the country. "Were I to answer all the letters I receive I should require half a dozen clerks," he wrote to a friend. The Government sat tight, because it did not wish to advertise the book by taking action. Moreover, the work was dedicated to the President of the United States in these words: "I present you a small Treatise in defence of those principles of Freedom which your exemplary Virtue hath so eminently contributed to establish." And as the British Government happened at that moment to be negotiating commercial treaties with General Washington, it was policy to ignore Paine.

The reception of the book in America was peculiar. It infuriated the Vice-President, John Adams, who as a monarchist always saw red when Paine's name was mentioned. It delighted the Secretary of State, Jefferson, who as a republican agreed with Paine throughout. It made Washington feel uncomfortable because he wished to rid America of British garrisons and saw no way of doing so but by a commercial treaty favorable to Great Britain. He was therefore in close communication with British agents, all of whom naturally expressed amazement that a pamphlet so offensive to the English Government should have been dedicated to the President. His discomfort was not decreased when Jefferson, Madison, and Randolph, wishing to strike a decisive blow for republicanism, urged him to give Paine a place in his Cabinet; and the situation was not eased when he heard from Paine: "As I have got the ear of the Country, I shall go on, and at least shew them, what is a novelty here, that there can be a person beyond the reach of corruption." He must also have devoutly echoed the prayer expressed by Paine in the same letter; "It is not natural that fame should wish for a rival, but the case is otherwise with me, for I do most sincerely wish there was some person in this Country that could usefully and successfully attract the public attention, and leave me with a satisfied mind to the enjoyment of quiet life: but it is painful to see errors and abuses and sit down a senseless spectator." Had Washington been something more than a good general and an able administrator, he would have given Paine a place in his Government; as it was, he sacrificed the man who, with himself, had created a republic, and flirted with the monarchy they had fought, writing to the author of *The Rights of Man* in those vague and noncommittal terms so characteristic of men who are famous for their foresight: "It is the first wish of my heart, that the enlightened policy of the present age may diffuse to all men those blessings to which they are entitled, and lay the foundation of happiness for future generations."

Paine was in Paris shortly after his book came out, arranging for its translation into French. There he witnessed the funeral procession of Mirabeau and heard Robespierre denounce capital punishment on the ground that no fallible human being should have the right to decree an irreparable sentence. Two blacks, Robespierre felt, did not make a white. He was later to prove that they made a red. Early in the morning of June 21, 1791, Lafayette rushed excitedly into Paine's bedroom

and cried, "The birds are flown!" As he was in charge
of the king and queen, their flight would seriously reflect upon him and he did not appreciate Paine's reply:
"'Tis well. I hope there will be no attempt to recall
them." But when the hue and cry was up and panic
measures were being taken, Paine drew the sensible
moral: "You see the absurdity of monarchical governments. Here will be a whole nation disturbed by the
folly of one man."

On June 25th he witnessed the return of the royal
pair, wondering why a nation which had been lucky
enough to lose a king should be so anxious to recover
him. His astonishment was so considerable that he forgot to put a cockade in his hat, and he had further cause
for surprise when the mob went for him with cries of
"*Aristocrat! À la lanterne!*" After an interval of maul-
ing that would have converted anyone else into a monarchist on the spot, he was saved by an English-speaking
Frenchman, to whom he explained his absence of mind
and who pacified the populace with the assurance that
Paine meant well. Having once been nearly lynched as
a spy in America and having just escaped hanging as an
aristocrat in France, Paine might have been excused for
entertaining a jaundiced view of the People. As it happened he helped to found a Republican Society within
a week of the latter event and to write its manifesto, in
which the king was promoted to the rank of a com-
moner, called for the first time Louis Capet, termed "a

political superfluity," and comforted with the assurance
that "France will not stoop to degrade herself by a
spirit of revenge against a wretch who has dishonoured
himself." This Society, which consisted of five members,
Paine, Achille Duchâtelet, Condorcet, Brissot, and
Nicholas Bonneville, caused a considerable stir. Even
the Jacobins at that time were against republicanism and
thought Paine too advanced. The royalists were of
course furious and demanded his prosecution. Nothing
happened; the storm blew over; and "Distinguished
Paine, the rebellious Needleman," as Carlyle called
him, left for England.

There is not much doubt that at intervals during the
next two or three years Paine was suffering from what
is commonly known as cerebral excitement. It had attacked him before, but the success of *Common Sense* and
*The Crisis* had been won in a field where competitors
were relatively few, while it was fairly generally admitted that *The Rights of Man* had not only floored the
most brilliant political thinker of the age but had
achieved a position unique in the literature of polemics.
He began to see himself as another Prometheus. He had
brought down the fire of heaven for man, but he was
chained to the rock of stupidity and attacked by the vul-
tures of cupidity. "I am the author of, I believe, one of
the most useful and benevolent books ever offered to
mankind," he would say in a chastened mood. But frequently such estimates appeared to him modest and he

would declare, with burning eyes and impulsive gestures, oblivious in his eagerness to the merits of his American publications, that if every book in the world were burned except *The Rights of Man*, humanity would greatly benefit by the bonfire. When people did not agree with him, he shrugged his shoulders in despair. He must try to save them in spite of themselves.

Back in London he wrote an "Address and Declaration of the Friends of Universal Peace and Liberty" which was read and adopted at a meeting of those optimists on August 20, 1791. He was still reputable enough to be popular with the advanced Whigs, and men like Horne Tooke, Godwin, Cartwright and Jebb were often in his company. They met regularly at the White Bear, Piccadilly,[1] and Paine's excitability was kept in check by the philosophic and cautious attitude of such men to public questions. Horne Tooke had been a practicing parson but had abandoned the practice and was now devoting himself to radical propaganda. This led him further than he meant to go and in 1794 he was tried for high treason. At his trial Cartwright affirmed that he had disapproved of certain parts of Paine's famous book, and another witness declared that he had consigned a letter, which he had been asked to forward to Paine, to the flames. He had been playing with fire and it was probably an inflammatory letter. After his acquit-

[1] The Criterion Restaurant stands on the site once occupied by the White Bear.

tal Tooke calmed down, but before the real trouble started he was one of Paine's closest associates.

Trouble was already beginning in the latter part of 1791. The Government was seriously concerned over the growth of societies advocating constitutional reform and had managed through its agents to influence the owners of taverns not to allow the use of their premises by "Painites." The principal villain of the piece determined to make the Government show its hand openly. "I have but one way to be secure in my next work," he told a friend, "which is to go further than in my first. I see that great rogues escape by the excess of their crimes, and perhaps it may be the same in honest cases." In November, 1791, he was the chief guest at a dinner given by the Revolution Society (founded to commemorate the Revolution of 1688) at the London Tavern. Many songs were sung on this occasion and many speeches made, including one by Paine in giving his toast "To the Revolution of the World."

On the whole, however, he led a quiet existence in the last months of 1791. He stayed with an old Lewes friend, a musician and bookseller, Thomas Clio Rickman, whose children were named after famous republicans, his eldest boy being called Thomas Paine Rickman. In this family Paine was as placid and contented as he could be. He wrote a lot, read very little, took a nap after dinner, and spent the evenings playing chess, draughts or dominoes, sometimes singing his own songs to Rickman's settings, sometimes talking until the early hours of the morning, when his eyes, "of which the painter could not convey the exquisite meaning," would become singularly luminous. Occasionally he visited friends or walked in the country or lounged in taverns, his favorite haunt being the White Bear. His circle of acquaintance was fairly extensive and included Lord Edward Fitzgerald, who was later to set Ireland ablaze; Romney, who was busy on a portrait of Paine; Sharp, who was afterwards to engrave the portrait; Stewart the walker; Priestley the talker, and the ambassadors of France and America. For the last time in his life his mind was at peace. The horrors of the future were hidden from him, the glories of the past gave him confidence; he was honored by those whose esteem he coveted and disliked by those whose aversion he valued. Life at the moment was extremely pleasant and the horizon was radiant with promise.

But this period of mental tranquillity was about to be disturbed by himself, for he was busy preparing a bomb, the explosion of which resounded throughout the civilized globe and shattered his peace forever.

## Chapter VIII

## THE WRONGS OF MEN

UNABLE to answer the arguments in *The Rights of Man*, the critics had concentrated on the grammar and were able to prove triumphantly that Paine had split his infinitives. The Government was less concerned with his syntax than with his opinions, and the moment it got wind of his intention to write a second installment it decided to square the publisher and queer the author. The method would have succeeded if Paine had been out for profit. Chapman, the publisher, offered one hundred guineas for the work when he first heard that Paine was writing it. In September, 1791, a large part of the manuscript was handed to Chapman, who then increased his offer to five hundred guineas. Later still he raised the sum to one thousand guineas for the copyright of the whole work. This would have given him the power to alter or suppress it and Paine refused the offer because he would not "treat as a mere matter of traffic that which I intended should operate as a principle." Chapman was of course simply acting as the tool of Government, Pitt and his satellites being feverishly anxious either to suppress the publication by bribing the publisher or to forestall Paine's criticism by reducing some of the taxes he censured.

The entire manuscript was in Chapman's hands six weeks before Parliament met, when Paine wanted the book to come out. Chapman's difficulty, since Paine had refused his offer, was to keep the book back until some weeks after the meeting of Parliament, when Pitt would have stolen Paine's thunder by making certain reductions in taxation suggested in the work. Unwittingly Paine himself helped Chapman out of the difficulty.

One day, a fortnight before the book was due from the press, Paine called on Mr. and Mrs. Chapman. He was a little intoxicated, having just dined with another publisher, and soon introduced his favorite topic when drunk—religion. Chapman was a dissenter but we do not know whether he took exception to Paine's views as a believer or as a bookseller. Probably the latter, because he must have known that contradiction affected his visitor like a blow on the face. At any rate, he managed to insult Paine, who rose in a fury, said that he had an extremely low opinion of dissenters, who were "all a pack of hypocrites," and stormed out of the house. Although Paine called the following morning to apologize for his behavior in front of Mrs. Chapman, the incident was useful to the publisher, who returned Paine's book at once, making it appear that he did not like to associate with so bad-mannered an author.

This meant a serious delay and the Second Part of *The Rights of Man* was published by Jordan in February, 1792, a fortnight after Parliament had assembled and Pitt had announced tax-relief on carts and wagons, on female servants, on candles, and on houses having under seven windows. "Every one of those specific taxes are a part of the plan contained in this work," wrote Paine in an appendix to his book, "and proposed also to be taken off." And he did not fail to point out how remarkable it was, in view of the multiplicity of taxes, that both Pitt and himself should have hit on the very same taxes at the very same time.

Part II of Paine's most famous work informed Lafayette, to whom it was dedicated, that "if you make a campaign the ensuing spring . . . I will come and join you. . . . I hope it will terminate in the extinction of German despotism, and in establishing the freedom of all Germany." Meanwhile he hoped by argument to extinguish British despotism and to establish freedom in England. In the preface he again dealt with Burke, who had not replied to Part I: "I am enough acquainted with Mr. Burke to know that he would if he could." Burke had, however, written an *Appeal from the New to the Old Whigs*, in which he had quoted largely from *The Rights of Man* but declined to answer it because it would probably be answered by others—"if such writings shall be thought to deserve any other reputation than that of criminal justice," he had added. Upon which Paine commented: "It must be *criminal* justice indeed that should condemn a work as a substitute for not being able to refute it."

So as to leave no one in two doubts as to the general tendency of his work, Paine introduced it in phrases that are not yet out-of-date. For example:

"I do not believe that the people of England have ever been fairly and candidly dealt by. They have been imposed on by parties and by men assuming the character of leaders."

"Could we suppose a spectator who knew nothing of the world, and who was put into it merely to make his observations, he would take a great part of the old world to be new, just struggling with the difficulties and hardships of an infant settlement. He could not suppose that the hordes of miserable poor with which old countries abound could be any other than those who had not yet had time to provide for themselves. Little would he think they were the consequence of what in such countries is called Government."

"The amazing and still increasing expences with which old Governments are conducted, the numerous wars they engage in or provoke, the embarrassments they throw in the way of universal civilization and commerce, and the oppression and usurpation they practice at home, have wearied out the patience and exhausted the property of the world."

"What is the history of all monarchical Governments but a disgustful picture of human wretchedness, and the accidental respite of a few years' repose? Wearied with war, and tired with human butchery, they sat down to rest, and called it peace."

"Almost everything appertaining to the circumstances of a Nation, has been absorbed and confounded under the general and mysterious word *Government*. Though it avoids taking to its account the errors it commits, and the mischiefs it occasions, it fails not to arrogate to itself whatever has the appearance of prosperity. It robs industry of its honours, by pedantically making itself the cause of its effects; and purloins from the general character of man, the merits that appertain to him as a social being."

Governments were, in short, a humbug and a nuisance:

"The instant formal Government is abolished, society begins to act: a general association takes place, and common interest produces common security."

He could produce proof of this:

"During the suspension of the old Governments in America, both prior to and at the breaking out of hostilities, I was struck with the order and decorum with which everything was conducted, and impressed with the idea that a little more than what society naturally performed was all the Government that was necessary, and that Monarchy and Aristocracy were frauds and impositions upon mankind."

Thus he was convinced that "The more perfect civilization is, the less occasion has it for Government, because the more it does regulate its own affairs, and govern itself."

In reviewing both old and new systems of government he dismissed monarchs in a sentence: "It requires some talents to be a common mechanic; but to be a King requires only the animal figure of man—a sort of breathing automaton." For hereditary rulers, too, one sentence was enough: "An hereditary governor is as inconsistent as an hereditary author. I know not whether Homer or Euclid had sons; but I will venture an opinion that if they had, and had left their works unfinished, those sons could not have completed them."

While dealing with the subject of constitutions he took the opportunity of asking a question that must have occurred to many people of a curious disposition: "How is it that the same persons who would proudly be thought wiser than their predecessors appear at the same time only as the ghosts of departed wisdom? How strangely is antiquity treated! To answer some purposes it is spoken of as the times of darkness and ignorance, and to answer others, it is put for the light of the world. If the doctrine of precedents is to be followed, the expences of Government need not continue the same. Why pay men extravagantly who have but little to do? If everything that can happen is already in precedent, legislation is at an end, and precedent, like a dictionary, determines every case. Either, therefore, Government has arrived at its dotage, and requires to be renovated, or all the occasions for exercising its wisdom have already occurred."

His own belief was in renovation: "Government ought to be as much open to improvement as anything which appertains to man, instead of which it has been monopolized from age to age, by the most ignorant and vicious of the human race. Need we any other proof of their wretched management, than the excess of debts and taxes with which every nation groans, and the quarrels into which they have precipitated the world? Just emerging from such a barbarous condition, it is too soon to determine to what extent of improvement Government may yet be carried. For what we can foresee, all Europe may form but one great Republic, and man be free of the whole." His sight must have been less hampered than ours, for we can say of new governments what he said of the old ones: "They pervert the abundance which civilized life produces to carry on the uncivilized part (war)." He gave an example of this: "If men will permit themselves to think, as rational beings ought to think, nothing can appear more ridiculous and absurd, exclusive of all moral reflections, than to be at the expence of building navies, filling them with men, and then hauling them into the ocean, to try which can sink each other fastest."

In a chapter entitled "Ways and Means of Improving the Condition of Europe" he showed where there was room for improvement: "There lies hidden from the eye of common observation, a mass of wretchedness that has scarcely any other chance, than to expire in poverty or infamy. Its entrance into life is marked with the presage of its fate; and until this is remedied, it is in vain to punish. . . . Why is it that scarcely any are executed but the poor? The fact is a proof, among other things, of a wretchedness in their condition. Bred up without morals, and cast upon the world without a prospect, they are the exposed sacrifice of vice and legal barbarity. The millions that are superfluously wasted upon Governments are more than sufficient to reform those evils, and to benefit the condition of every man in a Nation, not included within the purlieus of a Court." It was sheer cant to talk of civilization while such a state of things existed: "When it shall be said in any country in the world my poor are happy; neither ignorance nor distress is to be found among them; my jails are empty of prisoners, my streets of beggars; the aged are not in want; the taxes are not oppressive; the rational world is my friend, because I am the friend of its happiness: When these things can be said, then may that country boast its Constitution and its Government."

The many reforms he suggested included pensions

for people who had reached the age of fifty and he explained how easy it would be to save some of the money wasted on wars and spend it on this necessary provision. "It is painful to see old age working itself to death, in what are called civilized countries, for daily bread," he declared. Also pensions for people past fifty should not be given "as a matter of grace and favour, but of right." These words, let us remember, were written nearly a century and a half ago.

It was Paine's firm belief that the people of all countries had been prevented from thinking of their own condition by the glitter of monarchy, the glory of war and the glamor of religion, and as his remarks on these three subjects are as pregnant today as when he made them we may detach them from their contexts and set them down together:

"Every Ministry acts upon the same idea that Mr. Burke writes, namely, that the people must be hoodwinked, and held in superstitious ignorance by some bugbear or other; and what is called the Crown answers this purpose, and therefore it answers all the purposes to be expected from it."

"But any war is harvest to such Governments, however ruinous it may be to a nation. It serves to keep up deceitful expectations, which prevent a people looking into the defects and abuses of Government. It is the *lo here!* and the *lo there!* that amuses and cheats the multitude."

"What is called the present Ministry wish to see contentions about religion kept up, to prevent the Nation turning its attention to subjects of Government. It is, as if they were to say, 'Look that way, or any way, but this.'"

Paine almost certainly realized that he was asking for trouble when he wrote phrases like these, but he did not realize the extent of his personal danger and he did not anticipate the volume of vituperation that descended upon his head. He had reached a stage of mental exaltation which occurs in the lives of most saints, reformers, dictators, and gamblers, when the sense of reality is obliterated by a feeling of self-inflation. He honestly believed that with a blast from his trumpet the walls of evil would collapse. Alone he could do it. He was overwhelmed by a sensation of personal power and intoxicated by the vision of a new order evolved by himself.

"Should any person," he wrote to Jordan, "under the sanction of any kind of authority, enquire of you respecting the author and publisher of *The Rights of Man*, you will please to mention me as the author and publisher of that work, and shew to such person this letter. I will, as soon as I am made acquainted with it, appear and answer for the work personally."

An American whom we shall meet again, Gouverneur Morris, told him that he would be punished for his latest pamphlet. Paine laughed and said the Government dared not touch him: he was a national figure and could influence multitudes. "The disordered state of things in France works against all schemes of reformation both here and elsewhere," said Morris. Paine waved this aside: "The riots and outrages in France are nothing at all," he cried. "I shall not dispute it with you, as I am sure you do not mean what you say," replied Morris. But he did mean it, because his head was above the clouds and he only saw the stars.

The official world was slow to move and prepared the way by hiring a literary hack to write a scurrilous *Life* of Paine, in which the least pleasing aspects of his early years were laid before the public: the ill-treatment of his wife, the expulsions from the excise, and so on. When Paine heard of the projected *Life* of himself, he said of the author: "I wish that his own life and the lives of all the Cabinet were as good."

Gradually the feeling against him was worked up throughout the country. Patriotic resolutions were passed deploring the subversive opinions of madmen who would undermine the constitution and free the murderous instincts of criminals. The residents in Petty France, a thoroughfare in Westminster, decided to change its name to York Street "to perpetuate to posterity the detestation we, the said inhabitants, have to French principles, politics and all things that bear an affinity with the disordered system at present prevailing with that deluded people." When Paine heard this he remarked that "Fetter Lane" would have been a more reasonable substitute. Paragraphs began to appear in the newspapers calling attention to the wicked nature of certain writings that would "endanger our laws and liberties," meaning, as Paine pointed out, "endanger our places and pensions." Pitt, in private, admitted that "Tom Paine is quite right," but added: "What am I to do? As things are, if I were to encourage his opinions we should have a bloody revolution." Which, of course, would never do. Discipline had to be maintained; and so, when the situation was ripe for action, a summons was issued against Jordan, the publisher.

This was on May 14th, the book having had a run of about three months and having sold over fifty thousand copies. Paine was staying at Bromley in Kent when he heard the news, but instantly went to London, engaged a solicitor, and took upon himself all the expenses of the defense. Jordan, however, was not going to be shot at for Paine's sake and quickly sought the dugout of compromise. He agreed to appear in court, to plead guilty, and to hand over all his correspondence with the author concerning *The Rights of Man*. Having thus done his best to secure the conviction of Paine, he executed a strategic retreat and lived cautiously ever after.

On May 21st Paine received a summons at Rickman's house in Marylebone, and on the selfsame day, in order to influence the jury that would try the case, a royal proclamation against seditious writings was issued.

This, of course, stopped the sale of the book, as the public would not buy and the booksellers would not sell a work that exposed them to prosecution. In the indictment Paine was described firstly as a "gentleman," secondly as "a wicked, malicious, seditious, and ill-disposed person"; and he was accused of having said, among other things, that "The time is not very distant when England will laugh at itself for sending to Holland, Hanover, Zell, or Brunswick, for men" (meaning William III and George I) "at the expence of a million a year, who understood neither her laws, her language, nor her interest, and whose capacities would scarcely have fitted them for the office of a parish constable." Apparently this statement was an offense against the dignity of the Crown. The Home Secretary in Pitt's administration was Henry Dundas; and lest he should be in any doubt as to the author's feelings towards the reigning monarch, Paine wrote him a letter in which George III was referred to as "His Madjesty." A friend to whom Paine showed the letter objected to the pun. "Never mind," said Paine; "they say 'Mad Tom' of me, so I shall let it stand 'Madjesty.'"

The proclamation against seditious writings was followed by so many resolutions of devotion to the Crown from mayors and corporations and rotten boroughs all over the country that everybody felt the heart of the British People was sound, and when on June 8th Paine appeared in court to answer the charges against him the case was postponed until December. Already loyal citizens were publicly burning his works, but not before the less loyal portion of the community had purchased sufficient copies of his latest production for him to hand over £1,000 to the Society for Constitutional Information. A little later he was to be substituted for Guy Fawkes at the annual celebrations of the Gunpowder Plot, when a large number of stuffed Thomas Paines were ignited to the accompaniment of lusty cheers by drunken patriots. On hearing of these sacrificial orgies, he remarked: "A man who cries up king and constitution or church and state, or burns Tom Paine in effigy, may with impunity create as great riots as he pleases; but if a person attempts to show, by cool reasoning, that there are faults in the constitution, he shall be imprisoned for years and put on the pillory."

But these agreeable festivities did not take place until November, by which time he had been hounded out of the country. Throughout the summer months he was subjected to much personal inconvenience and he would probably have left for America if he had not determined to stand his trial. A number of hirelings were employed to hiss and hoot and hustle him whenever there was a likelihood of others joining in; several attempts were made to mob him, and if his face had been as familiar as his name William Cobbett might have been spared the trouble of bringing his bones back to England.

Paine quite rightly regarded these manifestations of

paid feeling as a sign of his growing importance. On August 26th the National Assembly in France conferred the title of "French citizen" upon him and early in September he was elected to the French Convention, the composition and calling of which he had proposed in Part I of *The Rights of Man*. He was unanimously chosen as deputy by three departments—Oise (Versailles), Puy-de-Dôme, and Pas-de-Calais—but he decided to sit for the last of these because it had elected him first. He received a letter, signed by thirty-three representatives of nine communes, acclaiming him in these words: "Your love for humanity, for liberty and equality, the useful works that have issued from your heart and pen in their defence, have determined our choice. It has been hailed with universal and reiterated applause. Come, friend of the people, to swell the number of patriots in an assembly which will decide the destiny of a great people, perhaps of the human race. The happy period you have predicted for the nations has arrived. Come! do not deceive their hope!" Another letter, from the President of the National Assembly, Hérault de Séchelles, declared that France called him to its bosom, because "it becomes the nation that has proclaimed the Rights of Man to desire among her legislators him who first dared to estimate the consequences of those Rights," and invited him to enjoy "the most interesting of scenes for an observer and a philosopher."

Paine did not require these incitements to desperate

action, but their effect on him was soon apparent. On
September 12th he attended a meeting of the "Friends
of Liberty" and in a state that would now be called
paranoiac he let forth a stream of "inflammatory eloquence." The next evening he was at the house of his
friend Johnson, the publisher, in St. Paul's Churchyard,
where he repeated what he had said to certain well-
wishers, among them the poet, William Blake, who,
however mystical in his writings, was realistic enough
in everyday matters. When Paine got up to go, Blake
rose too and, putting his hand on Tom's shoulder, said:
"You must not go home, or you are a dead man." Blake
showed extraordinary prevision, for the substance of
Paine's speech had been digested by the authorities, who
had already determined to act. The pleadings of his
friends, backed by the promptings of a Frenchman who
had been sent by the municipality of Calais to bring
him over, had the desired effect, and Paine left London
that night for Dover, going a round about way, through
Rochester, Sandwich, and Deal, in order to evade the
officers of the law, who had first gone to arrest him at
Rickman's house. At Dover the customs official was on
the lookout for suspicious characters and vigilantly attended to the luggage and pockets of Paine and his two
companions. Several letters in Paine's trunk would have
given the official courage if he had read them, for they
were from French republican bodies; but fortunately he
began with a letter from President Washington, in

which that warrior prayed for the happiness of future generations, and the sight of so famous a signature attached to so proper a sentiment produced a spasm of timidity in the breast of the official, whose curiosity was quickly suppressed. Paine was allowed to go on board, and twenty minutes after the packet had sailed two steaming horses came clattering through the streets of Dover. The warrant for Paine's arrest had arrived.

His arrest would merely have been the first step to his death, and for those who believed in divine interposition in the affairs of men it must have seemed that the Almighty had republican sympathies. Be that as it may, we must remain behind in monarchical England for a while and see what was done to Paine's reputation in default of his person.

For several months his countrymen amused themselves by burning effigies of "Tom Paine," made with straw and encased in stays, because the neighboring gentry paid more to see him in flames than they would have paid to see the Pope in a similar situation. The market-places of England, from Northumberland to Devonshire, were bright with such patriotic celebrations, the normal ritual commencing with a procession round the town, continuing with the erection of a gibbet from which the effigy hung for a period of pelting, and concluding with a purgatorial blaze, loud cheers, deep execrations and the singing of the National Anthem. As these rites were of so loyal a nature the authorities never interfered, and the worthy sentiments of the people received official sanction when the entertainments were rounded off with a burlesque trial of Paine for seditious libel in the Court of King's Bench on December 18, 1792, before Lord Kenyon and a special jury. The former being pensioned and the latter being packed, a verdict of guilty followed as a matter of course; but even had a fair hearing been possible the reading in court of a letter from Paine to the Attorney-General would have prejudiced the jury against him: "That the Government of England is as great, if not the greatest perfection of fraud and corruption that ever took place since governments began, is what you cannot be a stranger to; unless the constant habit of seeing it has blinded your sense. . . . Is it possible that you or I can believe that the capacity of such a man as Mr. Guelph, or any of his profligate sons, is necessary to the government of a nation? I speak to you as one man ought to speak to another. . . ."

Mr. Guelph was, of course, King George III; and as the counsel for the defense, Thomas Erskine, was Attorney-General to the eldest of Mr. Guelph's prodigal sons, the Prince of Wales, he was placed in rather a tricky position, from which he tried to escape by pretending that the letter was a forgery. Erskine made a fine speech in defense of free thought, free speech, and Thomas Paine, closing with the phrase, "I can reason with the people of England, but I cannot fight against the thunder of authority." The moment he sat down the

Attorney-General got up to reply, but as the jury had been paid for their verdict in advance, they naturally did not wish to waste any more time on the case, and the foreman intervened: "My Lord, I am authorized by the jury here to inform the Attorney-General that a reply is not necessary for them, unless the Attorney-General wishes to make it, or your Lordship." Neither of them expressing any desire to prolong the proceedings, the verdict of "Guilty" was given, Erskine's carriage was drawn in triumph by a mob that still preferred "mad Tom" to "His Madjesty," and Paine was henceforth outlawed from his native land.

But he had timed a bomb to burst after his departure. Among the documents in which the customs official had displayed an interest at Dover was a pamphlet replying to the loyal addresses which had been the only means the Government had discovered of answering *The Rights of Man.* This *Letter to the Addressers*, as it was called, explained that the prosecution of himself was due to the fact that cheap editions of his famous work had been issued, which meant that it was being read by the common people for whom it was written—"even children's sweetmeats being wrapped in it," as the Attorney-General complained at the trial. Paine went on to show how cases like his were prejudiced: the special jury was given a dinner and two guineas for a conviction, no dinner and one guinea for an acquittal. Some of his phrases in this pamphlet became proverbial:

"The project of hereditary Governors and Legislatures was a treasonable usurpation over the rights of posterity."

"When the rich plunder the poor of his rights, it becomes an example to the poor to plunder the rich of his property."

He bade farewell to Burke in a phrase that may perpetuate the memory of Burke:

"And the final event to himself has been, that, as he rose like a rocket, he fell like the stick."

He had been accused of libel, and this was his reply to the accusation:

"If to expose the fraud and imposition of monarchy and every species of hereditary government—to lessen the oppression of taxes—to propose plans for the education of helpless infancy, and the comfortable support of the aged and distressed—to endeavour to conciliate nations to each other—to extirpate the horrid practice of war—to promote universal peace, civilization, and commerce—and to break the chains of political superstition, and raise degraded man to his proper rank;—if these things be libellous, let me live the life of a libeller, and let the name of LIBELLER be engraven on my tomb!"

In spite of the legal conviction, the patriotic addresses and the popular burnings, the seed sown by *The Rights of Man* grew so quickly that the Government gave way to panic, and undertook to crush the book (in Hazlitt's words) "by a declaration of war against France to still the ferment, and excite an odium against its admirers, as taking part with a foreign enemy against their prince and country."

## Chapter IX

## CITIZEN CAPET

MEANWHILE "Deputy Paine, foreign Benefactor of the Species," as Carlyle described him, had been received with approval in France. When the boat arrived at Calais he was given a salute of guns from the fort and cheering crowds surged along the quay. As he stepped on shore the soldiers cleared a way and the officers stepped forward to embrace the popular deputy. The national cockade was stuck in his hat by a chosen damsel, the band struck up, and to shouts of *Vive Thomas Paine!* the procession moved towards the Town Hall, where he was embraced by the Mayor and all the municipal officers. A day of ceremonies and acclamations ended with a visit to the theater, where his box was ornamented with the words "For the Author of The Rights of Man."

He arrived at White's Hotel, Paris, on September 19, 1792, and two days later, when the Year One of the

Republic began, he was enthusiastically received in the Convention, which on the same day decreed the abolition of royalty in France. On September 25th he issued an "Address to the People of France," in which his hopes for the future were painted in roseate colors, but which ended on a note of caution: "In entering on this great scene, greater than any nation has yet been called to act in, let us say to the agitated mind, be calm. Let us punish by instructing, rather than by revenge." The facts concerning the prison massacres in the first week of that month were already leaking out and Paine was beginning to realize that the French citizenry were less amenable to discipline than his fellow-republicans on the other side of the Atlantic. Worse still, the Jacobin extremists in the Convention did not appear to be interested in such abstract ideals as the rights of man and their attitude to the principles of republicanism left much to be desired. "Revolutions are not made of rosewater," Danton warned him. "You believe in a republic!" Marat sardonically exclaimed. "Come, you have too much sense to believe in such a dream." And Robespierre, while listening with respect, frankly did not understand what he was talking about.

On October 11th a committee of nine was appointed to draft a constitution: Siéyès, Paine, Brissot, Pétion, Vergniaud, Gensonné, Barère, Danton, Condorcet. Of these constitutionalists none but Siéyès and Paine survived the Terror, Siéyès by keeping pace with the times,

Paine by refusing to adapt his views to any emergency and also by luck. As usual in politics, the important thing was treated with scant respect by the energetic and ambitious party, which was working up a crisis and preparing a coup out of a relatively insignificant matter. The Jacobins did not care a centime about a constitution, but they were quite willing to allow the Girondists to waste their time and expend their energy in drawing one up, because it amused them and kept them out of mischief. Meanwhile the Jacobins themselves were arousing popular feeling against the king, for they saw a good chance of coming into power over his dead body. They knew the Girondists would oppose the death penalty and would seal their own doom by their opposition. Their mouthpiece, Paine, had already said "It is the kingly *office*, rather than the officer, that is destructive"; and when congratulating the Convention on the abolition of royalty he had remarked: "Amid the joy inspired by this event, one cannot forbear some pain at the folly of our ancestors, who have placed us under the necessity of treating seriously the abolition of a phantom." In other words, the Girondists were not going to take the king seriously as a man, while the Jacobins were going to take him seriously enough to cut off his head and then accuse the Girondists of royalist sympathies.

When the time was ripe the Jacobins sprung their mine. The king's private safe was discovered in the Tuileries on November 20th (or perhaps the discovery had been unannounced until the time was ripe) and the documents therein were considered as proofs of the monarch's treachery. The mob were unleashed to yell for the death of "Capet," and Paine sat down in his lodging to check the blood lust of a people and to plead for the life of a king. His fellow-lodger at this time was Lord Edward Fitzgerald, who wrote to his mother: "I lodge with my friend Paine—we breakfast, dine, and sup together. The more I see of his interior, the more I like and respect him. I cannot express how kind he is to me; there is a simplicity of manner, a goodness of heart, and a strength of mind in him, that I never knew a man before possess." The three qualities mentioned by Fitzgerald were necessary at such a moment and are visible in the letter Paine addressed to the President of the Convention on the night of November 20th, which, "on account of my inability to express myself in French," was read to the deputies the following day. It was written with the object of insuring delay, so that the momentary outburst of rage against Louis should not lead to precipitate action. As always, Paine was fighting the principle, not the person, the monarchy, not the man. He made it clear that Louis should be tried, because he was probably part of a conspiracy of "crowned brigands" against liberty, and in trying him the institution of monarchy throughout Europe would be arraigned. But the implication throughout the letter was that Louis, "a

This statue, by Gutzon Borglum, shows Paine in the French National Assembly pleading for the life of Louis XVI. It was erected in Paris on January 29, 1937, a memorial to Paine on the 200th anniversary of his birth

weak and narrow-minded man, badly reared," was not personally responsible for his actions, and might therefore be shown "some compassion."

Apart from his natural humanitarianism Paine realized that it would be bad policy to execute Louis, whose death would be followed by foreign invasion. Also he knew that killing a monarch would not kill monarchy. His letter impressed the Convention and it was ordered to be printed; but the Jacobins were not to be curbed by reason and agitated for a decree of execution. Attempts were made by royalists to influence the leading revolutionaries and Danton said he would try to save the king if he could have "a million of money to buy up the necessary votes," the money to be handed over within eight days, but "I warn you," he added, "that although I may save his life I shall vote for his death; I am quite willing to save his head, but not to lose mine." Pitt was asked for the money, but refused it, preferring to spend it on the war which followed the execution of Louis. Thus the only Englishman who tried to save the king was the only Englishman who had been outlawed for disbelieving in kings. "If the French kill their king," said Paine, "it will be a signal for my departure, for I will not abide among such sanguinary men." But his abhorrence of monarchy was not lessened by the possibility of such an event, for while deploring the bloodthirstiness of the Jacobins he was writing to a backsliding friend in England: "What, then, means this sudden attachment to *kings?* this fondness of the English Government, and hatred of the French? If you mean to curry favour, by aiding your Government, you are mistaken; they never recompence those who serve it; they buy off those that can annoy it, and let the good that is rendered it be its own reward."

The Jacobins having failed to obtain their decree of execution, the trial of the king commenced on December 11th. The Girondists attempted to shirk their responsibility by urging an appeal to the people. Robespierre, fearing an outburst of popular sympathy with the king, opposed the appeal from motives of policy. Paine, fearing a continuance of popular hatred, opposed the appeal from motives of humanity. Again the mob were given the freedom of the streets and the Convention was paralyzed by an invasion of the "many-headed multitude." On January 15, 1793, Louis was unanimously voted guilty, and the attempt of the Girondists to make an appeal to the people was frustrated. The nature of the punishment had now to be decided, and Paine made another effort to save the king.

"I am inclined to believe that if Louis Capet had been born in obscure condition," he informed the Convention, "had he lived within the circle of an amiable and respectable neighbourhood, at liberty to practise the duties of domestic life, had he been thus situated, I cannot believe that he would have shown himself destitute of social virtues." The Constituent Assembly ought never to have restored Louis to the throne after his flight. "I was in Paris at the time of the flight . . . and when he was taken and brought back. The proposal of restoring him to supreme power struck me with amazement. . . . When I reflect on the unaccountable folly that restored the executive power to his hands . . . I am far more ready to condemn the Constituent Assembly than the unfortunate prisoner Louis Capet. But abstracted from every other consideration, there is one circumstance in his life which ought to cover or at least to palliate a great number of his transgressions, and this very circumstance affords to the French nation a blessed occasion of extricating itself from the yoke of kings, without defiling itself in the impurities of their blood. It is to France alone, I know, that the United States of America owe that support which enabled them to shake off the unjust and tyrannical yoke of Britain. . . . But as the nation at that time, restrained by the shackles of her own government, could only act by the means of a monarchical organ, this organ—whatever in other respects the object might be—certainly performed a good, a great action. Let then those United States be the safeguard and asylum of Louis Capet. There, hereafter, far removed from the miseries and crimes of royalty, he may learn from the constant aspect of public prosperity, that the true system of government consists not in kings, but in fair, equal and honourable representation. In relating this circumstance, and in submitting this proposition, I consider myself as a citizen of both countries. I submit it as a citizen of America, who feels the debt of gratitude which he owes to every Frenchman. I submit it also as a man, who, although the enemy of kings, cannot forget that they are subject to human frailties. I support my proposition as a citizen of the French republic, because it appears to me the best, the most politic measure that can be adopted." If Louis were killed his brothers would gain foreign support; there would be more bloodshed; "and it is our duty as legislators not to spill a drop of blood when our purpose may be effectually accomplished without it. It has already been proposed to abolish the punishment of death, and it is with infinite satisfaction that I recollect the humane and excellent oration pronounced by Robespierre on that subject in the Constituent Assembly. This cause must find its advocates in every corner where enlightened politicians and lovers of humanity exist, and it ought above all to find them in this assembly. Monarchical governments have trained the human race, and inured it to the sanguinary arts and refinements of punishment; and it is exactly the same punishment which has so long shocked the sight and tormented the patience of the people, that now, in their turn, they practise in revenge upon their oppressors. But it becomes us to be strictly on our guard against the abomination and perversity of monarchical examples: as France has been the first of European nations to abolish royalty, let her also be the first to abolish the punishment of death, and to find out a milder and more effectual substitute."

At eight o'clock in the evening of January 16th the voting on the question of punishment began, and went on for thirty-six hours. Long speeches were made by the deputies as they recorded their votes. The Jacobins had packed the galleries, which were full of half-drunk males and half-dressed females, who applauded those in favor of the death sentence and hissed those against it. Some of the leading Girondists, Vergniaud and Brissot among them, funked the issue at the last moment, played for safety and voted for death. Barère, who always had an eye to the main chance, frankly threw in his lot with Robespierre (whom he afterwards deserted at the right moment) by saying, "The tree of liberty does not grow if it be not watered with the blood of kings." Siéyès excused himself for joining the crowd with the words, "What were the tribute of my glass of wine in that torrent of brandy?" Paine stuck to his convictions: "I vote for the detention of Louis till the end of the war, and after that his perpetual banishment," he said, speaking in carefully-rehearsed French.

The scared majority favored death, and the question now was when should it take place? Here was Paine's last chance. If he could obtain delay he might yet save the king. The decision was to be taken on January 20th. His final appeal was made in the Convention the day before. The moment he mounted the tribune Marat guessed what was coming and determined to thwart the attempt. The speech, which was read in French by Deputy Bancal, began, "Very sincerely do I regret the Convention's vote of yesterday for death." Marat promptly interrupted: "I submit that Thomas Paine is incompetent to vote on this question. He is a Quaker; his mind is contracted by the narrow principles of his religion; he is incapable of the liberality requisite for condemning men to death." A great deal of confusion followed this statement. There were yells and counter-yells. The Jacobins were shocked to hear that Quakers could be so narrow-minded; and if Paine had not been an Englishman, and therefore excusably queer, he would not have been given a hearing. But after a pro-longed period devoted to cat-calling the assembly re-membered that free speech was one of the rights of man and Bancal was allowed to continue the reading of Paine's appeal, from which we may take a few pas-sages:

"My language has always been that of liberty *and* humanity, and I know that nothing so exalts a nation as the union of these two principles, under all circum-stances. I know that the public mind of France, and par-ticularly that of Paris, has been heated and irritated by the dangers to which they have been exposed; but could we carry our thoughts into the future, when the dangers are ended and the irritations forgotten, what today seems an act of justice may then appear an act of vengeance. [*Angry murmurs.*] My anxiety for the cause of France has become for the moment concern for her honour. If, on my return to America, I should employ myself on a history of the French Revolution, I had rather record a thousand errors on the side of mercy, than be obliged to tell one act of severe justice. . . .

"France has but one ally—the United States of America. That is the only nation that can furnish France with naval provisions, for the kingdoms of northern Europe are, or soon will be, at war with her. It unfortunately happens that the person now under discussion is considered by the Americans as having been the friend of their revolution. His execution will be an affliction to them, and it is in your power not to wound the feelings of your ally. Could I speak the French language I would descend to your bar, and in their name become your petitioner to respite the execution of the sentence on Louis."

Suddenly a Jacobin (Thuriot) shouted, "This is not the language of Thomas Paine."

Marat was quick to follow. Mounting the tribune, he asked Paine several questions in English. Upon Paine's assurance that the translation faithfully expressed his views, Marat jumped down and vehemently denounced the interpreter. "I assert that it is not Thomas Paine's opinion," he cried; "it is a false translation!"

"I have read the original, and the translation is correct," objected Deputy Garran.

Whereat further pandemonium. When it subsided Paine, still standing in the tribune beside Bancal, announced that the sentiments were his. The reading then proceeded:

"Your Executive Committee will nominate an ambassador to Philadelphia; my sincere wish is that he may announce to America that the National Convention of France, out of pure friendship to America, has consented to respite Louis. That people, by my vote, ask you to delay the execution. Ah, citizens, give not the tyrant of England the triumph of seeing the man perish on the scaffold who had aided my much-loved America to break his chains."

Beside himself with fury, Marat "launched himself into the middle of the hall" and screamed: "Paine voted against the punishment of death because he is a Quaker," which fact apparently determined the immorality of the vote. Paine answered, "I voted against it from both moral and political motives."

Next day Marat let loose his jackals; the deputies who might have favored delay were intimidated by the howls of the mob for "justice"; and Louis was sentenced to die within twenty-four hours.

There is little doubt that the British Ministry could have saved the French king, for in order to keep England neutral the Convention would have granted Pitt almost any favor he had cared to ask. But, as Brissot pointed out, "the grievance of the British Cabinet against France is not that Louis is in judgment, but that Thomas Paine wrote *The Rights of Man*." Something had to be done to divert the mental disquietude caused by that book, so Pitt followed the advice given by Henry IV to his son in Shakespeare's play:

> Be it thy course to busy giddy minds
> With foreign quarrels.

Troops were marched to London, Parliament was reassembled at short notice, the garrison of the Tower was reinforced, supplies were voted, Burke made a melodramatic gesture against France with the help of a stage dagger, and Fox felt impelled to ask Pitt, "Can you not prosecute Paine without an army?"

*Chapter X*

---

A DISILLUSIONED IDEALIST

---

IT IS generally overlooked that there was a reign of terror in England during the Reign of Terror in France, the difference being that in England it was directed against the books of one man, while in France it was directed against the lives of many. People who talked Paine, read Paine, or sold Paine were fined and imprisoned or transported. One Thomas Muir, who had advised people to read what the Lord Advocate described as "the works of that wretched outcast Paine," was sentenced to fourteen years' transportation. The sentence was received with hisses in court, and when the tipstaff was ordered to arrest the hissers he plaintively announced, "My lord, they're all hissing." There were dozens of such convictions. Town-criers were told to inspect bookshops and report street-corner conversation. The Bolton crier, having completed one of his rounds, reported that nowhere had he been able to find either

the rights of man or common sense. The public burnings, carried out at the orders of the gentry and more
respectable tradesmen, did not represent the true feeling
of the common people, who looked upon the business
as an excuse for a beano. Following the destruction of
one Paine effigy, a number of well-meaning yokels asked
their employer whether he would like "any other gem-
man burnt for a glass o' beer." There was a brisk trade
in shoe nails, the heads of which were shaped "T.P."
The tavern loafers and brothel loungers who bought
them would lift their legs and display the soles of their
boots explaining that they were "trampling on Thomas
Paine and his principles."

While the English were indulging in this campaign
of fear, the victim of their fury was saving the lives of
Englishmen in Paris. The British ambassador, Lord
Gower, had been recalled after the establishment of the
Republic and Paine was the only man left in France who
had the power to help his distressed countrymen. "His
vocation will not be complete," wrote Lord Fortescue of
Paine, "till his head finds its way to the top of a pike."
The heads of many citizens of the country that abused
him in this fashion just missed finding their way to the
top of a pike because he was there to save them. The
Girondists were still in power and placed him on the
Committee of Surveillance; he was therefore in a posi-
tion to succor his enemies. One of the latter, named
Munro, who had wondered how a nation could demean

itself by electing "such a fellow" as Paine to its Convention, was discovered in Paris after England's declaration of war, and immediately arrested. Paine obtained his release and safe departure. Another, Captain Grimstone, got into an argument with Paine during a dinner party. Paine was explaining the merits of republicanism and the demerits of monarchy, when Grimstone suddenly called him a traitor. Paine good-humoredly treated this as evidence of the fact that the Captain had been out-argued. Whereupon Grimstone proved Paine's point by striking him violently. Paine was fifty-six years of age; the Captain was a young man; and the Frenchmen present demanded that he should be executed for the crime of striking a deputy. He was seized and hurried off to prison, while Paine went straight to Barère, procured the freedom of Grimstone, a passport, and gave him money to leave the country quickly.

A third example is still more noteworthy because it happened after the fall of the Girondists, when Paine's influence had gone and his own life was in danger. An employee of the Birmingham firm of Boulton and Watt, Zachariah Wilkes by name, was arrested and condemned to death. He was innocent of offense and, having no friend in Paris to help him, he begged the jailer to lay his written statement before the President of the Convention. "No, my friend," answered the jailer; "my head is as good as yours and looks as well between the shoulders, to my liking," and he suggested that Wilkes should send his statement to Deputy Paine. "O God!" exclaimed Wilkes, "he must hate and detest the name of Englishman; pelted, insulted, persecuted, plundered!" Nevertheless it seemed his only chance, so he handed the paper containing proof of his innocence to the jailer, who took it to Paine. Within half an hour Paine was at the prison and Wilkes informed him that he had documents of the greatest importance for his employers, James Watt and Matthew Boulton, and that not only his life but his reputation was in question.

"I know your employers by report only," said Paine; "there are no two men less favorable to the principles I profess, but no two upon earth are honester. You have only one great man among you: it is Watt; for Priestley is gone to America. The church-and-king men would have japanned him."

He then examined Wilkes closely, and having satisfied himself of the man's innocence he declared:

"The leaders of the Convention would rather have my life than yours. If by any means I can obtain your release on my own security, will you promise me to return within twenty days?"

"Sir," answered Wilkes, "the security I can at present give you is trifling—I should say a mere nothing."

"Then you do not give me your word?"

"I give it and will redeem it."

Paine went away, but returned the same evening, and, with a penetrating look, addressed the other as follows:

"Zachariah Wilkes! if you do not return in twenty-four days (four are added) you will be the most unhappy of men; for had you not been an honest one, you could not be the agent of Watt and Boulton. I do not think I have hazarded much in offering to take your place on your failure; such is the condition."

Wilkes was speechless. Paine remained calm. The jailer broke the silence with the words, "He seems to get fond of the spot now he must leave it," for the prisoner was overcome with emotion and remained for some time unable to move.

"Zachariah!" said Paine, "follow me to the carriage," and they went out between a file of soldiers, who saluted the deputy.

Wilkes returned in due course and Paine greeted him with the remark, "There is yet English blood in England." Later Wilkes regained his liberty and lived to tell this story. He was one of many who owed their lives to Paine, the friends of whom were being persecuted in England.

After the execution of the king it is almost certain that Paine would have left France if he had not been hopeful that the Constitution, on which he was still working with Condorcet, would become law. As it was a Girondist undertaking, the Jacobins were determined to prevent this, and on the very day that had been set apart for its discussion they launched their attack on the Girondists by demanding the arrest of their leaders, on the ground that they were royalists, tyrants, traitors, reactionaries, and all the other things that men are usually called when another set of men wish to take their places. The attack had been preceded by a circular, signed by Marat as President of the Jacobin Club, in which it had been proposed that the Girondist deputies should be exterminated. Whereupon the Convention, in which the Girondists had a majority, decreed the arrest of Marat. He appeared before the Revolutionary Tribunal, was acquitted, and became the hero of the hour.

Although their first attempt to arrest the Girondist leaders failed, the Jacobins, with the mob at their beck and call, daily gained strength in the Convention, and when the Constitution came up for discussion Robespierre had no difficulty in sidetracking it by arguing that the Declaration of Rights which dealt with generalities and which had also been largely drafted by Paine, should be discussed first. For the Jacobins there was of course only one form of government—themselves—and the Constitution as framed by Paine and Condorcet would have placed them in a state of inactivity. When at length it was debated, Robespierre hit on an omission which obviously had not occurred to Paine and made great capital out of the fact that the Deity was not mentioned. As there is no subject in the world about which human beings get so excited as the next world, Robespierre's way was clear. He became the champion of the Supreme Being, identified him with

Nature, and gave him the attributes of Robespierre. The
next thing to be done was to draw up another Constitution. The Jacobin Club was equal to the occasion; it
produced one in a week; and this, like the first, was
shelved until the country was in a fit condition to appreciate it.

But some months before the Jacobins produced their
Constitution the two parties in the Convention were engaged in a deadly fight for supremacy. Paine was, of
course, on the side of the moderate Girondists, among
whom he numbered many friends, especially Brissot
and Condorcet. This meant that he had incurred the
hostility of the Jacobin Club, and from the moment he
tried to save the king's life Marat hated him. "Frenchmen are mad to allow foreigners to live among them,"
said Marat. "They should cut off their ears, let them
bleed a few days, and then cut off their heads." Marat's
enmity brought about a tragic episode in connection with
Paine. There was a young Englishman named Johnson
whose admiration of Paine was such that he had followed the outlaw to Paris. Upon hearing that Marat
intended to denounce his hero, Johnson in despair tried
to commit suicide, after leaving all his property to
Paine in a will. The attempt failed, and at a later date
Paine was able to save the young man's life, but the
incident affected him deeply. Life was indeed becoming
more and more unbearable for a man of his idealistic
nature. Already, in April, 1793, he was beginning to

abandon hope for humanity. Liberty had become the mask on the hideous face of anarchy. A deep note of depression sounded in his letters to American friends, and early in May he sat down with a heavy heart to write a last appeal to Danton:

"I am exceedingly disturbed at the distractions, jealousies, discontents and uneasiness that reign among us, and which, if they continue, will bring ruin and disgrace on the Republic. . . . I now despair of seeing the great object of European liberty accomplished, and my despair arises not from the combined foreign powers, not from the intrigues of aristocracy and priestcraft, but from the tumultuous misconduct with which the internal affairs of the present revolution is conducted." He gave Danton some good advice on government and trade, and then touched the root of the trouble: "I am distressed to see matters so badly conducted, and so little attention paid to moral principles. It is these things that injure the character of the Revolution and discourage the progress of liberty all over the world. . . . There ought to be some regulation with respect to the spirit of denunciation that now prevails. If every individual is to indulge his private malignancy or his private ambition, to denounce at random and without any kind of proof, all confidence will be undermined and all authority be destroyed. Calumny is a species of Treachery that ought to be punished as well as any other kind of Treachery. It is a private vice productive of public evils; because it is possible to irritate men into disaffection by continual calumny who never intended to be disaffected. It is therefore equally as necessary to guard against the evils of unfounded or malignant suspicion as against the evils of blind confidence. It is equally as necessary to protect the characters of public officers from calumny as it is to punish them for treachery or misconduct." Finally he referred to the list of Girondists who had been denounced by the Jacobins: "Most of the acquaintances that I have in the convention are among those who are in that list, and I know there are not better men nor better patriots than what they are."

Paine also wrote Marat a letter which, unfortunately, has not been preserved. One cannot assume that an appeal for humanity touched the heart of the chief Jacobin, but something in the letter must have made his intelligence function, because Paine and Condorcet, the authors of the republican Constitution, were not arrested with the Girondists on June 2nd.

Following the downfall of his friends, Paine found himself alone in the Convention, for even Condorcet made himself scarce when he saw which way the wind was blowing. The tragedy of Paine's solitude in the Convention was intensified by the feeling of loneliness that oppressed his soul. Fanaticism had triumphed over reason, anarchy over order; men, freed from the shackles of centuries, had forged new ones for themselves; the kingdom of benevolence had been conquered by the dark forces of enmity and jealousy; brotherly love had given way to fratricidal hate; ignorance had routed philosophy, passion had killed common sense, barbarism had displaced progress, and the blackness of despair had blotted out the bright hues of hope. Everything for which he had planned and fought, all his belief in mankind and faith in the future, had vanished like a dream. Man was incapable of liberty, of improvement. It was a ghastly awakening, a knock-out blow to his self-esteem. All the weary years of work for his fellow-creatures had been wasted. He could no longer believe in himself because he could no longer believe in Man. The ground was cut clean away from beneath his feet. It was for him the end of all things; and for weeks he found numbness, if not solace, in brandy. He stupefied himself with drink, trying to forget the loss of friends and ideals in the misty, shifting world created by alcohol.

With the murder of Marat by Charlotte Corday on July 13th came the first glimmer of fresh hope. Perhaps his successor would save the Girondists. Danton, in spite of his ferocity, had a heart. Robespierre, in spite of his coldness, had spoken against capital punishment. The country might yet get its Constitution. Paine forsook the bottle and took courage. By nature he was an optimist, and, like the man who has lost a fortune but suddenly sees a chance of retrieving a pittance, he was

able to persuade himself that things were not so bad as
they seemed. France was still the promised land, if not
the land of promise. Marat out of the way, all might
yet be well, for no one surely could be so bad as Marat.
But Paine was to learn soon enough that in crises the
majority of men do not differ greatly; they behave like
fools or criminals, according to their disposition at birth.
Until that last lesson he partially renewed his hopeful
view of the universe, and he did so in a setting well cal-
culated to comfort the afflicted and to restore confidence
in the human race.

After the fall of the Girondists there was still in
Paris a small group of unrepentant republicans, of
whom Paine was the leader. With the Terror hanging
over them a few of these clustered together under the
roof of an ancient mansion, once the residence of
Madame de Pompadour, at No. 63 Faubourg St.-
Denis. Here, through the summer weeks of 1793,
Paine talked and wrote letters and walked in the garden and received his friends and acted as a sort of unofficial ambassador for Englishmen in trouble, and
enjoyed himself as much as possible under the circumstances. The mansion was surrounded by a wall; it
stood well back from the street and resembled a farm-
house, for turkeys, geese, ducks, fowls, rabbits, and pigs
wandered about the courtyard, and Paine took pleasure
in feeding them from the parlor window on the ground
floor. At the rear of the house was a garden of more

than an acre, stocked with orange, apricot, and plum trees. The spot was some distance from the Convention, remote from the turmoils of the city, and enjoyed the tranquillity of the countryside.

Paine's own apartments consisted of three rooms, of which the sitting-room led through a glass door on to a small railed-in veranda, from which he could descend a narrow flight of stairs, nearly hidden by the vinetrees that grew over them, into the garden. His occupations did not vary much from day to day. He generally rose at about seven, breakfasted with his friends, and then spent an hour or two in the garden, at the upper end of which there was a broad gravel walk where these grave republicans would pass the time away "in those childish amusements that serve to keep reflection from the mind—such as marbles, Scotch hops, battledores, etc., at which we were all pretty expert," wrote Paine to a friend. These innocent pastimes were followed by work and he would spend the time until dinner in his sitting-room, writing perhaps to Robespierre on the scarcity of salt-peter or to the Committee of Public Safety on the European alliance against France. Sometimes he went out to dine with a friend, but usually he stayed at home with his fellow-boarders, telling anecdotes of the past, playing chess, whist, piquet, cribbage, or discussing the news of the day which their landlord had just brought from the city.

He seldom went to the Convention, because he could

not associate himself with the "tremendous decrees" of
the Jacobins and found it useless and dangerous to oppose them. He had been a marked man from the moment he had spoken against the sentence on the king,
and no one would translate or read aloud any opinion
he might have dared to express. "My heart was in distress at the fate of my friends," he confessed later, and
"I used to find some relief by walking alone in the garden, after dark, and cursing with hearty good will the
authors of that terrible system that had turned the
character of the Revolution I had been proud to
defend."

So long as there was any chance of saving his
Girondist friends he maintained official relations with
Robespierre, and it is probable that Robespierre pretended a respect for his opinions until the Terror commenced in grim earnest, for in the days ahead Paine
summed up the leading Jacobin as a hypocrite. In spite
of his unusual sagacity, judgment, and foresight in social and political matters, Paine lacked intuition in his
personal dealings with men. "Every circumstance," he
was able to say, "is pregnant with some natural effect,
upon which intentions and opinions have no influence;
and the political error lies in misjudging what the effect
will be"; which was only half true. His own weakness
lay in under-rating the effect of personality on the se-
quence of events. He persistently misjudged men because
he thought them like himself and never allowed for the

jealousy, envy, malice, greed, and stupidity which form the larger part of most people's spiritual make-up. Men of all sorts could impose upon him if their vocal sentiments seemed unexceptionable. The result was a series of disillusionments, from none of which did he profit, followed by a number of judgments which were distorted in proportion as he had been duped. Burke, Robespierre, Washington, and Napoleon provide the more obvious examples of his inability to estimate character. He admired them all at first, partly, no doubt, because they expressed admiration for him, and Burke and Washington aroused his bitterest hostility because he believed they had deceived him more completely than the other two.

But his most serious miscalculation of the human factor in governing events very nearly cost him his life; for while the Paris of that day was furnishing him with sufficient evidence of human bestiality to shock a Swift, he did not even realize that a man whom he had made to look a fool might nurse a grudge against him.

## Chapter XI

---

### THE HUMAN ELEMENT

---

GOUVERNEUR MORRIS was the American minister to France from 1792 to 1794. He had known Paine in the United States and neither had taken to the other. Temperamentally they were poles apart. Morris, a royalist and *bon viveur*, was far more interested in wine and women than in revolutions and constitutions. He was one of those fat, complacent, friendly, cheerful people who are usually taken at their face value, who are given a license denied to their thinner and graver brethren, and whose comfortable appearance, disarming manners, easy-going disposition, and freedom of speech so often mask less agreeable spiritual qualities. Moreover, Morris, as a result of a carriage accident at the age of twenty-eight, had lost a leg, and a fat man with a wooden leg who maintains his cheerfulness is practically suspicion-proof. He was popular wherever he went; and although he asserted that he would "doubtless be a steadier man with one leg than with two," his career of gallantry was not noticeably subdued by the absence of a natural limb. In fact, during his stay in London, just before his appointment as minister to France, he spent much time in studying the art of sex appeal. "In the course of conversation," he noted in his diary, "my sister tells me that the fashionable style for young men in London is to affect great *ennui*, and receive advances from the ladies which they hardly deign to notice."

Like so many of those smug and podgy folk of whom he was a type, he was exceptionally vain, and few things annoyed him so much as the boasting of others. Paine's high opinion of himself and his writings disgusted Morris, whose envy and malice are apparent in almost every reference he made to Paine in his diary. Disagreement between them started in America over the Silas Deane affair. Morris fancied himself as a financial expert—indeed he practically founded the national coinage of America—and he did not relish Paine's exposure of Deane, in whom he believed. He therefore urged Paine's dismissal from the office of Secretary to the Foreign Affairs Committee. When the truth came to light he veered with characteristic rapidity, "hopped around on one leg," Paine reported, "swore that they all had been duped, himself among the rest, complimented me on my quick sight, and by God, says he, nothing carries a man through the world like honesty."

Morris was in the confidence of President Washing-

ton, for whom he carried on delicate negotiations with
the British Government, and although Paine did not
know this at the time, he was annoyed when Morris
was sent as minister to Paris, because he knew of the
man's royalist sympathies and was afraid the appointment would not tend to a closer understanding between
France and the United States. Being in the habit of
speaking his thoughts, he mentioned his regret to Morris, who took it in good part and registered a black
mark against him. Beneath an exterior of charm and
good-nature these black marks invisibly accumulated,
and every time that Paine opened his heart to the dis-
ingenuous minister he unconsciously fed an enmity
which at length became murderous.

It must be admitted that there were some irritating
moments for Morris. Throughout the latter part of
1792 and the first half of 1793 Paine's position in the
Convention gave him a diplomatic prestige that eclipsed
his fellow-countryman's. When Genêt was sent as minister to the United States, Morris was not informed of
the appointment, but Paine was. Shortly after this a
serious breach occurred in their relationship. A number
of American ships containing cargoes for France were
captured by British cruisers. As a result French cruisers
were ordered to capture American ships bearing cargoes
to any port in Europe, and in a little while ninety-two
captured American ships were lying idle at Bordeaux,
being forbidden to load up again and depart in case the

English should capture them. Morris was delighted
with this violation of the treaty between France and
America, because he wanted it broken and in its place a
treaty between England and America. He therefore
contented himself with reporting the violation to the
French and American Governments, trusting that this
would cause bad blood and terminate the commercial
agreement between the two countries, and took no notice of the plea by the captains of the vessels that he
should arrange their departure.

The captains then applied for help to Paine, who
made it his business to call on Morris and demand why
he had done nothing to assist his countrymen. Morris
apparently replied that he had done all that was necessary; at which Paine flared up and asked, "Do you not
feel ashamed to take the money of the country and do
nothing for it?" Describing this incident in a letter,
Morris accused Paine of trying to step into his shoes
and of being besotted with drink from morning to night.
The first statement was untrue, for Paine not only urged
Barère to treat Morris with respect because of the
proved patriotism of his kinsmen in America, but de-
plored the possibility of his removal or resignation from
office on account of the anti-French feeling he would
generate if he returned home. The second statement
was true, for at that time Paine was passing through
his brandy phase.

Some weeks later the captains had an interview with

Morris, who informed them "that they had thrown
themselves into the lion's mouth, and it was for them
to get out of it as best they could." Again they fell back
on Paine, to whom they suggested a public protest
against the American minister's inaction. Paine argued
them out of this and recommended instead an appeal to
the Convention. This was successful and the captains
were permitted to depart. It was a bitter pill for Morris
to swallow. Not only had Paine done what was really
the minister's job and made Morris look silly into the
bargain, but he had saved the treaty between France
and America. A very large black mark was duly registered.

But it was now high time that some of these scores
should be paid off, and Morris got to work. As it happened, Genêt, the French minister in America, had been
dabbling in local politics over there, and, incurring the
dislike of Washington, had been recalled. It also happened that Deforgues, the French Minister of Foreign
Affairs, was anxious to take the place of Genêt in America. Morris turned both occurrences to account. Genêt
had been intimate with Paine and the Girondists. Deforgues could not succeed Genêt without the help of
Morris. How easy, then, to use Deforgues to damn
Paine! By associating Paine with Genêt's interference
in American affairs, by asserting that the powers in
America were angry with such meddling, and by hint-
ing that Paine as a native of England was probably

conspiring against both countries, Morris was able to convince Deforgues that the friend of Genêt and the Girondists was a danger to the state. Action followed quickly. On October 3, 1793, Paine was included in the denunciation of the Girondists, read to the Convention behind locked doors. On October 31st the Girondists were guillotined, their twenty-one heads falling in thirty-eight minutes. In December Paine was denounced for his friendship with the dead men and for his intrigues with Genêt. There followed a resolution to exclude foreigners from every public function during the war. In spite of his French citizenship Paine was treated as a foreigner—indeed the resolution was directed at him—and this brought him under a law passed in June whereby aliens of hostile nations were imprisoned. On December 28th the author of *The Rights of Man* was under lock and key.

From the first week of October, when the Girondists were formally accused, Paine had known his time was short, and had been preparing what he thought would be his last testament to the human race. With an odd inappropriateness he called it *The Age of Reason*. As the days darkened over the old house in the Faubourg St.-Denis he sat in his sitting-room, from which he could see both garden and courtyard, and wrote out the thoughts which had been germinating in his mind for many years. As a rule, his method when writing a book was to compose sentences and paragraphs in his head while out walking, and on his return to write them down, never afterwards altering them. But now he was in a hurry and was forced to set himself doggedly at a table, writing for hours on a stretch. Fortunately his thoughts for this work were fairly well arranged. He had always meant to attack the superstition of the Church just as he had attacked the superstition of the State; but the need to proclaim his beliefs had become greater within the last few years because to many people atheism seemed the only alternative to superstition, and both were obnoxious to him. So, with the knife of the guillotine suspended over his neck, he wrote out his confession of faith.

Though deep in his work and in hourly danger of arrest, he never failed to help his few remaining friends with money, advice, and the remnants of power attached to his office. By procuring passports in the nick of time he managed to get his young disciple Johnson and another friend out of France. "Two days after they were gone I heard a rapping at the gate, and looking out of the window of the bedroom I saw the landlord going with the candle to the gate, which he opened; and a guard with muskets and fixed bayonets entered. I went to bed again and made up my mind for prison, for I was the only lodger. It was a guard to take up Johnson and Choppin, but, I thank God, they were out of their reach."

While aiding two other fellow-countrymen he received a visitor whose call and considerate offer would have made a more timid man apprehensive: "I went into my chamber to write and sign a certificate for them, which I intended to take to the guardhouse to obtain their release. Just as I had finished it, a man came into my room, dressed in the Parisian uniform of a captain, and spoke to me in good English and with a good address. He told me that two young men, Englishmen, were arrested and detained in the guardhouse, and that the section (meaning those who represented and acted for the section) had sent him to ask me if I knew them, in which case they would be liberated. This matter being soon settled between us, he talked to me about the Revolution, and something about *The Rights of Man*, which he had read in English; and at parting offered me, in a polite and civil manner, his services. And who do you think the man was who offered me his services? It was no other than the public executioner, Samson, who guillotined the king and all who were guillotined in Paris, and who lived in the same street with me."

By the middle of December a silence had fallen on the mansion in the Faubourg St.-Denis. The poultry and the pigs were still there, but Paine was the only human boarder, for even his landlord had been arrested. "I appeared to myself to be on my death bed," he said, "for death was on every side of me, and I had no time to lose." He wrote at high pressure; and though all his famous works, *Common Sense, The Crisis,* and *The Rights of Man,* had also been written under the stress of emergency, none was more clearly and concisely expressed than this one, produced by a man whose "friends were falling as fast as the guillotine could cut their heads off" and whose own fate seemed as certain as theirs. Like some reformers before and since his time, he saw his own strivings and fate prefigured in the character of Jesus Christ, in writing of whom he was writing of himself:

"Nothing that is here said can apply, even with the most distant disrespect, to the *real* character of Jesus Christ. He was a virtuous and an amiable man. The morality that he preached and practised was of the most benevolent kind; and though similar systems of morality had been preached by Confucius, and by some of the Greek philosophers, many years before, by the Quakers since, and by many good men in all ages, it has not been exceeded by any. . . . That such a person as Jesus Christ existed, and that he was crucified, which was the mode of execution at that day, are historical relations strictly within the limits of probability. He preached most excellent morality, and the equality of man; but he preached also against the corruptions and avarice of the Jewish priests, and this brought upon him the hatred and vengeance of the whole order of priesthood. The accusation which those priests brought against him was that of sedition and conspiracy against

Before he was imprisoned for his objections to the Reign of Terror, Paine gave the manuscript of *The Age of Reason* to a friend for safe-keeping. He had finished the work six hours before his arrest

the Roman Government, to which the Jews were then subject and tributary; and it is not improbable that the Roman Government might have some secret apprehension of the effects of his doctrine as well as the Jewish priests; neither is it improbable that Jesus Christ had in contemplation the delivery of the Jewish nation from the bondage of the Romans. Between the two, however, this virtuous reformer and revolutionist lost his life."

Paine finished his work six hours before he was arrested. To simplify matters he went back for one night to his old lodgings at White's Hotel, which was still his official residence as a deputy, where the arrest took place; and for safety's sake he handed his manuscript to a friend, Joel Barlow. Apparently it was necessary in France, as in England, to mobilize all the forces of the country in order to deal with Thomas Paine. "The [British] Government was obliged to suspend the Constitution, and to go to war to counteract the effects of his popularity," wrote Hazlitt; and in order to make certain of his arrest the Committee of General Surety in Paris empowered its officers to "ask the help of the Civil authorities, and, if need be, of the army." The only other foreign deputy affected by the recent resolution of the Convention was Anacharsis Cloots, who was taken on the same day with Paine to the Luxembourg. Cloots had been famous as "the orator of the human race" and was soon to be guillotined on a false charge. The officers who arrested Paine treated him with respect, and the concierge of the Luxembourg, Benoit, "a man of good heart, shewed to me every friendship in his power, as did also all his family, while he continued in that station."

After he had been in prison about three weeks, all the Americans then in Paris went to the Convention in a body to reclaim their friend and countryman. Their appeal, however, was not sanctioned by Gouverneur Morris, the representative of the United States Government, and in his reply the President of the Convention asserted that Paine was "a native of England" and that their application was "unofficial." Paine and his friends at once tried to make it "official" by appealing to Morris to claim him as an American citizen. But Morris was equal to the occasion. Having got his enemy safely immured, he was not going to risk a release while the situation was under his control; so he hatched a nice little plot with the French Minister of Foreign Affairs. With the help of a letter written to him by Deforgues, it would appear that he had unsuccessfully claimed Paine as an American citizen and that Paine was claimed as a French citizen by the Government of France. It did not occur to the conspirators that as Paine had been imprisoned because he was an Englishman his continued incarceration was irregular from the moment his French citizenship was acknowledged. However, no one was going to worry over technical trivialities of that kind, and Morris was able to convince not only the Americans in Paris, but such leading Americans in Philadelphia as Jefferson, Washington, and Edmund Randolph that he had done everything possible in Paine's behalf. He even emphasized the importance of not agitating for Paine's release, as the slightest false step might prove fatal. Thus advised by their own minister on the spot, the American Government remained quiescent, and Morris's plan to get rid of Paine lay concealed for nearly a century, until the discovery of his correspondence with Deforgues.

In the innocence of his heart Paine wrote from prison to Morris: "You must not leave me in this situation. . . . You know I do not deserve it. . . . I apply to you as the Minister of America, and you may add to that service whatever you think my integrity deserves."

Morris answered this appeal by informing Robespierre that he could not acknowledge Paine's right to pass as an American. Morris had not been made to look a fool for nothing.

*Chapter XII*

---

THE AGE OF REASON

---

WHILE Paine is paying the penalty of teaching another man how to do his job properly, let us glance at the work he has been writing in the shadow of death. As it was instantaneously condemned, root and branch, by every pious body, as it was regarded by every secular authority as seditious and pernicious, as its author was hated and anathematized and branded as an atheist in every civilized country by every Christian community, the modern reader will not need to be told that it was a profoundly religious book. Paine believed that it was sacrilege to call the Bible the Word of God, that the Almighty could not be so circumscribed; and naturally he was censured for blasphemous obscenity, which was the current terminology for blunt honesty. Voltaire had already used the rapier of wit in the same cause; Paine seized the bludgeon of common sense and delivered a series of shattering blows on the skull of theology. It was the first serious frontal attack, all along the line, on organized Christianity, and the Christians disliked it so much that they accused him of using poison gas. Let us try a whiff or two.

"I believe in one God, and no more; and I hope for happiness beyond this life," were almost his opening words. "I believe the equality of man, and I believe that religious duties consist in doing justice, loving mercy, and endeavouring to make our fellow-creatures happy."

"I do not believe," he continued, "in the creed professed by the Jewish church, by the Roman church, by the Greek church, by the Turkish church, by the Protestant church, nor by any church that I know of. My own mind is my own church. All national institutions of churches, whether Jewish, Christian, or Turkish, appear to me no other than human inventions set up to terrify and enslave mankind, and monopolize power and profit. I do not mean by this declaration to condemn those who believe otherwise; they have the same right to their belief as I have to mine. But it is necessary to the happiness of man, that he be mentally faithful to himself. Infidelity does not consist in believing or in disbelieving; it consists in professing to believe what he does not believe. It is impossible to calculate the moral mischief, if I may so express it, that mental lying has produced in society. When a man has so far corrupted and prostituted the chastity of his mind, as to subscribe his professional belief to things he does not

believe, he has prepared himself for the commission of
every other crime. He takes up the trade of a priest for
the sake of gain, and, in order to qualify himself for
that trade, he begins with a perjury. Can we conceive
anything more destructive to morality than this?"

With a passing reference to "the adulterous connection of Church and State," he then dealt with revela-
tions: "The Jews say that their Word of God was given
by God to Moses face to face; the Christians say, that
their Word of God came by divine inspiration; and the
Turks say, that their Word of God (the Koran) was
brought by an angel from heaven. Each of those
churches accuses the other of unbelief; and, for my part,
I disbelieve them all." The way to God was open to
every man alike, he declared. "No one will deny or dispute the power of the Almighty to make such a communication if he pleases. But admitting, for the sake of
a case, that something has been revealed to a certain
person, and not revealed to any other person, it is revelation to that person only. When he tells it to a second
person, a second to a third, a third to a fourth, and so
on, it ceases to be a revelation to all those persons. It is
revelation to the first person only, and *hearsay* to every
other, and, consequently, they are not obliged to believe
it. It is a contradiction in terms and ideas to call anything a revelation that comes to us at second hand, either
verbally or in writing."

After mentioning some of the origins of the Christian

mythology, he described the fable of the Fall of Man
in these terms: "He (Satan) is then introduced into the
garden of Eden in the shape of a snake, or a serpent,
and in that shape he enters into familiar conversation
with Eve, who is no ways surprised to hear a snake talk;
and the issue of this tête-à-tête is, that he persuades her
to eat an apple, and the eating of that apple damns all
mankind." Of this and similar episodes he remarked:
"The more unnatural anything is, the more is it capable
of becoming the object of dismal admiration."

From his examination of the Old Testament we may
take the following:

"Whenever we read the obscene stories, the voluptu-
ous debaucheries, the cruel and torturous executions,
the unrelenting vindictiveness, with which more than
half the Bible is filled, it would be more consistent that
we called it the word of a demon, than the Word of
God. It is a history of wickedness, that has served to
corrupt and brutalize mankind; and, for my own part,
I sincerely detest it, as I detest everything that is cruel.

"When I see throughout the greatest part of this
book scarcely anything but a history of the grossest
vices, and a collection of the most paltry and contemptible tales, I cannot dishonour my Creator by calling it
by His name."

He passed on to an examination of the New Testament, from which "the church has set up a system of
religion very contradictory to the character of the per-

son whose name it bears. It has set up a religion of pomp and revenue in pretended imitation of a person whose life was humility and poverty."

It was, in Paine's view, the belief in the doctrine of redemption that debased the moral character of man: "It is by his being taught to contemplate himself as an out-law, as an out-cast, as a beggar, as a mumper, as one thrown as it were on a dunghill, at an immense distance from his Creator, and who must make his approaches by creeping, and cringing to intermediate beings, that he conceives either a contemptuous disregard for everything under the name of religion, or becomes indifferent, or turns what he calls devout. In the latter case, he consumes his life in grief, or the affectation of it. His prayers are reproaches. His humility is ingratitude. He calls himself a worm, and the fertile earth a dunghill; and all the blessings of life by the thankless name of vanities. He despises the choicest gift of God to man, the Gift of Reason; and having endeavoured to force upon himself the belief of a system against which reason revolts, he ungratefully calls it *human reason*, as if man could give reason to himself. Yet, with all this strange appearance of humility, and this contempt of human reason, he ventures into the boldest presumptions. He finds fault with everything. His selfishness is never satisfied; his ingratitude is never at an end. He takes on himself to direct the Almighty what to do, even in the government of the universe. He prays dictatorially. When it is sunshine, he prays for rain, and when it is rain, he prays for sunshine. He follows the same idea in everything that he prays for; for what is the amount of all his prayers, but an attempt to make the Almighty change his mind, and act otherwise than he does? It is as if he were to say—thou knowest not so well as I."

St. Paul was "a manufacturer of quibbles," and the "book of enigmas" called *Revelation* required a revelation to explain it. What, then, was the true Revelation? "The Word of God is the Creation we behold: and it is this word, which no human invention can counterfeit or alter, that God speaketh universally to man. . . . In fine, do we want to know what God is? Search not the book called the scripture, which any human hand might make, but the scripture called the Creation."

Belief in God might be difficult, but disbelief was impossible: "The only idea man can affix to the name of God, is that of a *first cause*, the cause of all things. And incomprehensively difficult as it is for a man to conceive what a first cause is, he arrives at the belief of it, from the tenfold greater difficulty of disbelieving it. It is difficult beyond description to conceive that space can have no end; but it is more difficult to conceive an end. It is difficult beyond the power of man to conceive an eternal duration of what we call time; but it is more impossible to conceive a time when there shall be no time. In like manner of reasoning, everything we behold carries in itself the internal evidence that it did not make itself. Every man is an evidence to himself, that he did not make himself; neither could his father make himself, nor his grandfather, nor any of his race; neither could any tree, plant, or animal make itself; and it is the conviction arising from this evidence, that carries us on, as it were, by necessity, to the belief of a first cause eternally existing, of a nature totally different to any material existence we know of, and by the power of which all things exist; and this first cause, man calls God. . . .

"Almost the only parts in the book called the Bible, that convey to us any idea of God, are some chapters in Job, and the 19th Psalm; I recollect no other. Those parts are true *deistical* compositions; for they treat of the Deity through his works. They take the book of Creation as the word of God; they refer to no other book; and all the inferences they make are drawn from that volume. . . . I recollect not a single passage in all the writings ascribed to the men called apostles, that conveys any idea of what God is. Those writings are chiefly controversial; and the gloominess of the subject they dwell upon, that of a man dying in agony on a cross, is better suited to the gloomy genius of a monk in a cell, by whom it is not impossible they were written, than to any man breathing the open air of the Creation."

The Christian system of faith appeared to Paine as "a species of atheism, a sort of religious denial of God. It professes to believe in a man rather than in God. It is a compound made up chiefly of man-ism with but little deism, and is as near to atheism as twilight is to darkness. It introduces between man and his Maker an opaque body, which it calls a redeemer, as the moon introduces her opaque self between the earth and the sun, and it produces by this means a religious, or rather an irreligious, eclipse of light. It has put the whole orbit of reason into shade. . . . That which is now called natural philosophy, embracing the whole circle of science, of which astronomy occupies the chief place, is the study of the works of God, and of the power and wisdom of God in his works, and is the true theology . . . and it is not among the least of the mischiefs that the Christian system has done to the world, that it has abandoned the original and beautiful system of theology, like a beautiful innocent, to distress and reproach, to make room for the hag of superstition. . . . The Almighty lecturer, by displaying the principles of science in the structure of the universe, has invited man to study and to imitation. It is as if he had said to the inhabitants of this globe that we call ours, 'I have made an earth for man to dwell upon, and I have rendered the starry heavens visible, to teach him science and the arts. He can now provide for his own comfort, and learn from my munificence to all, to be kind to each other.' "

Paine traced the effects of Christianity on education and the attempts made by the Church to stop the prog-

ress of thought and scientific discovery. He sketched the
system of the universe and showed the absurdity of explaining it by the myth of Eden or the story of Christ:
"From whence then could arise the solitary and strange
conceit that the Almighty, who had millions of worlds
equally dependent on his protection, should quit the
care of all the rest, and come to die in our world, because, they say, one man and one woman had eaten an
apple! And, on the other hand, are we to suppose that
every world in the boundless creation had an Eve, an
apple, a serpent, and a redeemer? In this case, the person who is irreverently called the Son of God, and sometimes God himself, would have nothing else to do than
to travel from world to world, in an endless succession
of death, with scarcely a momentary interval of life."

Some people had averred that even though the Bible
story were a pious fraud, it had been productive of good.
Paine refused to accept this: "It is with a pious fraud as
with a bad action, it begets a calamitous necessity of
going on. . . . From the first preachers the fraud went
on to the second, and to the third, till the idea of its
being a pious fraud became lost in the belief of its being
true; and that belief became again encouraged by the
interest of those who made a livelihood by preaching it."

All down the ages the people had been deceived by
Mysteries and Miracles. But "mystery is the antagonist
of truth. It is a fog of human invention that obscures
truth, and represents it in distortion. Truth never in-

velops *itself* in mystery; and the mystery in which it is at any time enveloped, is the work of its antagonist, and never of itself. . . . As *mystery* answered all general purposes, *miracle* followed as an occasional auxiliary. The former served to bewilder the mind, the latter to puzzle the senses. The one was the lingo, the other the legerdemain." As for the evidence for miracles, "We have never seen, in our time, nature go out of her course; but we have good reason to believe that millions of lies have been told in the same time; it is, therefore, at least millions to one, that the reporter of a miracle tells a lie."

According to Paine, the most extraordinary miracle related in the New Testament was that of Satan taking Christ to the top of a high mountain and showing him and promising him all the kingdoms of the earth. Our author treated this incident in the flippant manner that so much irritated his critics: "How happened it that he did not discover America? or is it only with kingdoms that his sooty highness has any interest? I have too much respect for the moral character of Christ to believe that he told this whale of a miracle himself. . . . It requires, however, a great deal of faith in the devil to believe this miracle."

In any case miracles had proved nothing and had merely turned religion into a trade requiring advertisement: "Instead of admitting the recitals of miracles as evidence of any system of religion being true, they ought to be considered as symptoms of its being fabulous. It is necessary to the full and upright character of truth that it rejects the crutch; and it is consistent with the character of fable to seek the aid that truth rejects.

At the close of the book Paine reasserted his faith in a future life: "I trouble not myself about the manner of future existence. I content myself with believing, even to positive conviction, that the power that gave me existence is able to continue it, in any form and manner he pleases, either with or without this body; and it appears more probable to me that I shall continue to exist hereafter than that I should have had existence, as I now have, before that existence began."

Finally he declared the sectarian differences in men's beliefs to be unimportant: "It is certain that, in one point, all nations of the earth and all religions agree. All believe in a God. The things in which they disagree are the redundancies annexed to that belief; and therefore, if ever an universal religion should prevail, it will not be believing anything new, but in getting rid of redundancies, and believing as man believed at first. Adam, if ever there was such a man, was created a Deist; but in the mean time, let every man follow, as he has a right to do, the religion and worship he prefers."

## Chapter XIII

AN UNREASONABLE AGE

THERE was an interesting succession of callers at the Luxembourg prison, all of whom were passing through it on their way to the scaffold. One of them, Deforgues, was partly responsible for Paine's discomfiture, but as neither could speak the language of the other, Paine remained in ignorance of Morris's treachery. Hérault de Séchelles, who as President of the National Assembly had told Paine that France called him to its bosom, here left him for the guillotine. Camille Desmoulins and Anacharsis Cloots bade him an everlasting farewell, and Danton said good-by with the words: "That which you did for the happiness and liberty of your country, I tried in vain to do for mine." General O'Hara, who had fought against America, was a fellow-prisoner for a time, and when he was released Paine lent him £300. This sum, which was Paine's total capital at the time, had been hidden by him in the lock of his cell-door.

For months he remained in suspense with no news from the outside world. "There was no time when I could think my life worth twenty-four hours," he wrote, "and my mind was made up to meet its fate." Frequently he heard the screams and tearful protestations of the men and women dragged out to die. One night in July, 1794, a hundred and sixty-nine people were taken from the prison, tried the following morning, and all but nine executed the same day. In the midst of such scenes, and not knowing when his own turn would come, Paine began to write the second part of *The Age of Reason*, which he read to a Brighton surgeon named Bond, who spent much time in his cell during the daytime and on bidding him good-night often wondered whether he would be alive the following morning. His continued existence, as the months went by, was indeed a little curious. It was almost certainly due to the fact that Robespierre did not trust Morris and did not wish to offend Washington. He knew that Paine and Washington were friends; he knew that Morris and Washington were friends; he guessed that Paine and Morris were enemies; so he waited to see whether Washington would move on behalf of Paine. As we know, Washington had been wrongly informed of the circumstances by Morris, and therefore he did nothing. Having allowed sufficient time for Washington to act, had he wished to do so, Robespierre decided that Paine had better complete his journey to the guillotine and wrote the fatal words: "*Demander que Thomas Payne soit décréte d'accusation, pour les intérêts de l'Amerique autant que de la France.*" The "interests of America" were of course the "interests of Morris" and we know quite enough about that plausible minister to sense his prompting behind the demand of Robespierre.

Short of the direct intervention of Providence, Paine was now a dead man. But just as he had been saved from the clutches of Pitt, so was he spared from the doom of Robespierre; which almost made it appear, in spite of overwhelming evidence to the contrary provided by the Christian sects, that the Almighty was a deist.

It so happened that Paine was ill with a fever when Robespierre's command should have been executed and was temporarily unaware of his miraculous escape. His illness was severe; for long periods he was unconscious; and it was thought that he could not recover. He was attended with unremitting zeal by his three cell-companions, by two fellow-prisoners (Bond, the aforesaid surgeon, and Dr. Graham, a physician), and by the prison doctor, Marhaski, to all of whom he paid tribute in his next publication. After his partial recovery, some two months later, he learned that Robespierre had fallen and how it had come about that he himself was still alive:

"The room in which I lodged was on the ground floor, and one of a long range of rooms under a gallery, and the door of it opened outward and flat against the wall; so that when it was open the inside of the door appeared outward, and the contrary when it was shut. I had three comrades, fellow prisoners with me, Joseph Vanheule of Bruges, Charles Bastini, and Michael Robyns of Louvain. When persons by scores and by hundreds were to be taken out of the prison for the guillotine it was always done in the night, and those who performed that office had a private mark or signal by which they knew what rooms to go to, and what number to take. We, as I have said, were four, and the door of our room was marked, unobserved by us, with that number in chalk; but it happened, if happening is the proper word, that the mark was put on when the door was open and flat against the wall, and thereby came on the inside when we shut it at night; and the destroying angel passed by it."

Some years later Barère apologized to Paine for having signed his death warrant, saying that he had been obliged to do so to save his own neck. Paine, who was brave enough himself to sympathize with the cowardice of other people, accepted the apology and subsequently did Barère a good turn.

For a man of Paine's interest in public affairs the greatest deprivation of prison life was lack of news; and if it had not been for Benoit he would have been cut off entirely from the outside world. But with the help of this kindly jailer he received sympathetic letters from a friend, Lady Smith, which lightened his misery; and his correspondence with her consoled him during the first few months, until Benoit was arrested, a man named Gayard was made keeper, and terror reigned in the Luxembourg.

After the execution of Robespierre efforts were again made by one or two friends to get Paine released, and he was persuaded to send a personal appeal to the Convention. "Ah, my friends," he wrote, "eight months' loss of Liberty seems almost a life-time to a man who has been, as I have been, the unceasing defender of Liberty for twenty years." But as this appeal was forwarded to the Committee of Public Safety, which did not number Liberty among its aims, it never reached the Convention. Also Morris was still American minister and he had no desire to receive a personal visit from Paine.

But help was at hand. In August, James Monroe succeeded Morris as minister and heard, to his amazement, that Paine was in prison. He immediately approached Deforgues' successor, a man named Buchot, who was so nervous that Morris declared he dared not wipe his nose without the permission of the Committee of Public Safety. Buchot twittered his concern and asked Monroe whether he had brought instructions from his Government for Paine's release as an American citizen. Naturally he had not, because his Government had assumed that Morris was dealing with the case.

Meanwhile Paine got to hear that Monroe was in

Paris and managed with the assistance of the prison lamp-lighter, to smuggle a letter through to him. Monroe promptly sent back a message assuring Paine of his friendship and promising to do everything in his power to help. Paine then wrote a long Memorial setting forth his claim to American citizenship, and still he did not realize that Morris had been responsible for his arrest and long imprisonment. Monroe replied with a letter of sympathy and encouragement. "It is unnecessary for me to tell you," wrote the future President of the United States, "how much all your countrymen, I speak of the great mass of the people, are interested in your welfare. They have not forgotten the history of their own revolution, and the difficult scenes through which they passed; nor do they review its several stages without reviving in their bosoms a due sensibility of the merits of those who served them in that great and arduous conflict. The crime of ingratitude has not yet stained, and I trust never will stain, our national character. You are considered by them as not only having rendered important services in our own revolution, but as being on a more extensive scale the friend of human rights, and a distinguished and able advocate in favor of public liberty. To the welfare of Thomas Paine the Americans are not and cannot be indifferent. Of the sense which the President has always entertained of your merits, and of his friendly disposition towards you, you are too well assured to require any declaration of it from me.

That I forward his wishes in seeking your safety is what I well know; and this will form an additional obligation on me to perform what I should otherwise consider as a duty." Monroe also assured Paine that there was no doubt about his American citizenship and begged him to face his situation "with patience and fortitude" until his freedom could be obtained.

Innumerable difficulties cropped up at every step taken by Monroe to secure Paine's release. Morris had not yet left France and his friends on the Committee of Public Safety continually put obstacles in the way of his successor. However, he vanished from the scene in the latter part of October, to spend some time as toady in turn to George III and Louis XVIII, and on November 2, 1794, Monroe called the attention of the Committee of General Surety to the fact that Paine was languishing in prison, and suggested that as the services he had "rendered to his country in its struggle for freedom have implanted in the hearts of his countrymen a sense of gratitude never to be effaced as long as they shall deserve the title of a just and generous people," early action on their part would be advisable.

This did the trick. On November 4th, Citizen Thomas Paine was set at liberty, after an imprisonment on no specific charge of over ten months. He had aged considerably in that time. A severe abscess had formed in his side, as a result of his illness in prison; he was often in great bodily pain; his constitution was irretrievably impaired; he stooped; the brightness had gone from his eyes; he walked wearily; and his hair was white. Monroe and his wife took the careworn and embittered man, who looked ten years older than he was, into their home, and tried to nurse him back to physical health and spiritual tranquillity.

The French authorities were now anxious to make reparation, and while England was joyfully reading a broadsheet containing "the last dying words of Thomas Paine, Executed at the Guillotine," France was recalling him "to the bosom of the Convention" and offering him a pension for having "deserved well of the human race, and consecrated liberty in the two worlds." Paine declined the pension, but accepted the invitation of the Convention, writing for that body a "Dissertation on First Principles of Government," which included this memorable warning: "An avidity to punish is always dangerous to liberty. It leads men to stretch, to misinterpret and to misapply even the best of laws. He that would make his own liberty secure, must guard even his enemy from oppression; for if he violates this duty, he establishes a precedent that will reach to himself." To join in the debate on a new Constitution Paine made what was, after his imprisonment, his first and last appearance in the Convention. The Constitution that had been submitted disfranchised about half the nation; and Paine, who had not yet grasped the fact that all movements for the amelioration of society merely end with the amelioration of a class, made a last appeal for the Rights of Man. He ascended the tribune with difficulty and stood there, a frail bent figure, while another man read his speech in French. His final words to a nation which had suffered so much for liberty, and was soon to suffer much more for abandoning it, should be remembered: "If you subvert the basis of the Revolution, if you dispense with principles and substitute expedients, you will extinguish that enthusiasm which has hitherto been the life and soul of the revolution; and you will substitute in its place nothing but a cold indifference and self-interest, which will again degenerate into intrigue, cunning, and effeminacy." But his words were wasted on the Convention, which was more concerned with prolonging its own existence than with granting the country a wise Constitution. Shortly it was displaced by the Directory, which in turn gave way to a Dictator; and the same had happened before, and the same is happening now, and the same will always happen until the world is peopled with Paines.

Monroe had no cause to regret his kindness and hospitality, for Paine's advice and help proved invaluable and Monroe's dispatches owed much to the knowledge and experience of his invalid guest. The diplomatic exchanges relative to the free navigation of the Mississippi were largely inspired by Paine, and if it had not been for the somewhat shady commercial treaty which Washington patched up with Great Britain at about this time, and which aroused the indignation of France, Paine would once again have served the United States as he alone could.

But he had come out of prison a different man. Ten months without sufficient light, air, and exercise had weakened and wasted him. The abscess in his side, which was never completely cured, was a source of constant pain; physical exhaustion prostrated him at regular intervals, and sometimes it seemed, both to his host and himself, that he could not live much longer. "The prospect now is that he will not be able to hold out more than a month or two at the furthest," wrote Monroe to a relation, explaining that he could not leave Paris for St.-Germain on account of Paine's ill-health: "I shall certainly pay the utmost attention to this gentleman, as he is one of those whose merits in our Revolution were most distinguished." Some time before this was written Paine had felt a relapse coming on and had settled down to the completion of *The Age of Reason*, Part II, which he had begun in prison. Thus both parts of that work were composed in the face of death, though neither was regarded by his contemporaries as a praiseworthy dying confession. The general trend of criticism in his own day was to the effect that he was not a deist but a drunkard, and the popular feeling worked up against him in England and America manifested itself in a phrase: "The World, the Flesh, and Tom Paine." The grossest misrepresentations came, naturally, from his

clerical critics, though the Bishop of Llandaff (Dr. Rich-
ard Watson) was much fairer than might have been expected of a man who made a fat living out of Christianity.

Moncure Conway, in the course of his monumental
work on Thomas Paine, said that no reasonably intelligent person could suppose that the effect of *The Age of
Reason*, "on which book the thirty years' war for religious freedom in England was won, after many martyr-
doms, came from a scoffing or scurrilous work." It is
true to say that Paine was too serious a man to scoff for
the sake of scoffing and too anxious to argue people out
of their prejudices to be scurrilous for the sake of scur-
rility. "In writing upon this, as upon every other subject, I speak a language plain and intelligible," he said
in his reply to Bishop Watson. "I deal not in hints and
intimations. I have several reasons for this: first, that I
may be clearly understood; secondly, that it may be
seen I am in earnest; and thirdly, because it is an affront
to truth to treat falsehood with complaisance." All the
same he must have known that his style of controversy
would offend a great many people and he could not have
been ignorant of the fact that, in matters of belief,
bluntness was sure to be mistaken for blasphemy. No
man has ever gone about the work of conversion in a
less diplomatic fashion. In the preface to the second
part of his book he said that he had been unable to refer
to the Old and New Testaments when writing the first

part; "notwithstanding which I have produced a work
that no Bible Believer, though writing at his ease, and
with a library of Church Books about him, can refute."
His critics, however, would now find that he had fur-
nished himself with both Testaments; "and I can say
also that I have found them to be much worse books
than I had conceived." This was not the language of
conciliation.

Having taken care to antagonize every Christian sect
in the preface he tackled the Old Testament with a
vigor that must have irritated the Jews as well. After
noting that in the Books of Moses, Joshua, etc., the most
appalling crimes were committed at the express command of God, he declared that "to read the Bible without horror, we must undo everything that is tender,
sympathizing, and benevolent in the heart of man.
Speaking for myself, if I had no other evidence that
the Bible is fabulous, than the sacrifice I must make to
believe it to be true, that alone would be sufficient to
determine my choice." For this reason he announced:
"It is a duty incumbent on every true deist, that he
vindicates the moral justice of God against the calum-
nies of the Bible." Or, as he once said to a friend, "you,
by taking the Bible for your standard, will have a bad
opinion of God; and I, by taking God for my standard,
shall have a bad opinion of the Bible."

He then set himself the task of proving that the
books supposed to have been written by one man must

have been written by another. We cannot here follow his clear and forceful exposition, but some of his hits were so characteristic, revealing his personality so vividly, that they must be quoted. To take an example. The authorship of the Book of Numbers was commonly ascribed to Moses. But in that work the following appeared: "Now the man Moses was very meek, above all the men which were on the face of the earth." Upon which Paine commented: "If Moses said this of himself, instead of being the meekest of men, he was one of the most vain and arrogant coxcombs; and the advocates for those books may now take which side they please, for both sides are against them: if Moses was not the author, the books are without authority; and if he was the author, the author is without credit, because to boast of *meekness* is the reverse of meekness, and is *a lie in sentiment*."

The Book of Deuteronomy inspired this reflection: "Priests have always been fond of preaching up Deuteronomy, for Deuteronomy preaches up tythes."

The mass of contradictions, the obvious inaccuracies, the historical improbabilities, the chronological confusions, the tales of murder, massacre, rape, treachery, debauchery, and similar assortments of barbarity, were all displayed by Paine, stripped of their poetry and set down in naked prose. "I will not go out of the Bible for proof of the supposed authenticity of the Bible," he promised, and the burden of his narrative was contained in the words: "What can be greater blasphemy than to ascribe the wickedness of man to the orders of the Almighty!" His general feeling with regard to the early history of the Jews was summed up in this manner:

"Could we permit ourselves to suppose that the Almighty would distinguish any nation of people by the name of *his chosen people*, we must suppose that people to have been an example to all the rest of the world of the purest piety and humanity, and not such a nation of ruffians and cut-throats as the ancient Jews were—a people who, corrupted by and copying after such monsters and imposters as Moses and Aaron, Joshua, Samuel, and David, had distinguished themselves above all others on the face of the known earth for barbarity and wickedness. If we will not stubbornly shut our eyes and steel our hearts it is impossible not to see, in spite of all that long-established superstition imposes upon the mind, that the flattering appellation of *his chosen people* is no other than a LIE which the priests and leaders of the Jews had invented to cover the baseness of their own characters; and which Christian priests sometimes as corrupt, and often as cruel, have professed to believe."

The Book of Ruth came as a relief after the horrors of Moses and Joshua: "An idle, bungling story, foolishly told, nobody knows by whom, about a strolling country-girl creeping slily to bed to her cousin Boaz. Pretty stuff indeed to be called the word of God. It is, however, one of the best books in the Bible, for it is free from murder and rapine." But the best thing in the Old Testament was the Book of Job, no doubt because it did not properly belong to the Bible. It was not in any sense a Hebrew production. It was older than any book in the Old Testament, said Paine, "and it is the only one that can be read without indignation or disgust."

The character of Solomon provoked Paine to write what amounted to a personal confession. The poetry of the famous "Song" was entirely lost on him; it was "amorous and foolish enough"; and, if the Bible-makers were to be believed, it was written when Solomon was "in the honey-moon of one thousand debaucheries." As for the Book of Ecclesiastes, it consisted of "the solitary reflections of a worn-out debauchee . . . who looking back on scenes he can no longer enjoy, cries out *All is Vanity!* . . . Seven hundred wives, and three hundred concubines, are worse than none; and, however it may carry with it the appearance of heightened enjoyment, it defeats all the felicity of affection, by leaving it no point to fix upon; divided love is never happy. This was the case with Solomon; and if he could not, with all his pretensions to wisdom, discover it beforehand, he merited, unpitied, the mortification he afterwards endured. In this point of view, his preaching is unnecessary, because, to know the consequences, it is only necessary to know the cause. Seven hundred wives and three hundred concubines would have stood in place of the whole

book. It was needless, after this, to say that all was
vanity and vexation of spirit; for it is impossible to de-
rive happiness from the company of those whom we
deprive of happiness.

"To be happy in old age it is necessary that we accus-
tom ourselves to objects that can accompany the mind
all the way through life, and that we take the rest as
good in their day. The mere man of pleasure is miserable in old age; and the mere drudge in business is but
little better: whereas natural philosophy, mathematical
and mechanical science, are a continual source of tranquil
pleasure, and in spite of the gloomy dogmas of priests,
and of superstition, the study of those things is the study
of the true theology; it teaches man to know and to
admire the Creator, for the principles of science are in
the creation, and are unchangeable, and of divine origin.

"Those who knew Benjamin Franklin will recollect,
that his mind was ever young; his temper ever serene;
science, that never grows grey, was always his mistress.
He was never without an object; for when we cease to
have an object we become like an invalid in an hospital waiting for death."

Passing to the prophets, our commentator observed
that, though men believed what the prophets had said,
it did not appear that the prophets believed one another: "they knew each other too well." Jeremiah, ap-
propriately, drove him to despair. "This book, the
Bible," he exclaimed in a footnote, "is too ridiculous for

criticism." Further: "What then can we say of these prophets, but that they are impostors and liars?" The ignorance and superstition of modern times had "elevated those poetical, musical, conjuring, dreaming, strolling gentry, into the rank they have since had." And: "Were I, or any other man, to write in such a disordered manner, no body would read what was written, and every body would suppose that the writer was in a state of insanity."

One more quotation will show that Paine was not suckled on fairy-stories and that there was no room in his mind for the fantasies of imagination. Of Jonah and the whale he wrote: "A fit story for ridicule, if it was written to be believed; or of laughter, if it was intended to try what credulity could swallow; for, if it could swallow Jonah and the whale, it could swallow anything."

He concluded his survey of the Old Testament in that self-assured manner which made so many people keen to kick him: "I have now gone through the Bible, as a man would go through a wood with an axe on his shoulder, and fell trees. Here they lie; and the priests, if they can, may replant them. They may, perhaps, stick them in the ground, but they will never make them grow.—I pass on to the books of the New Testament."

His treatment of the New Testament was not so effective, though it was much more offensive. His account of the birth of Christ, which he described as "putting the story into intelligible language," would not pass a modern printer; and his opening assertion that "the New Testament compared with the Old, is like a farce of one act, in which there is not room for very numerous violations of the unities," was not sympathetic enough to induce his Christian readers to accompany him farther. Again, of course, he had no difficulty in producing a quantity of conflicting evidence, and there is a characteristic passage dealing with the circumstances of the crucifixion:

"The writer of the book of Matthew should have told us who the saints were that came to life again, and went into the city, and what became of them afterwards, and who it was that saw them; for he is not hardy enough to say that he saw them himself;—whether they came out naked, and all in natural buff, he-saints and she-saints, or whether they came full dressed, and where they got their dresses; whether they went to their former habitations, and reclaimed their wives, their husbands, and their property, and how they were received; whether they entered ejectments for the recovery of their possessions, or brought action of *crim. con.* against the rival interlopers; whether they remained on earth, and followed their former occupation of preaching or working; or whether they died again, or went back to their graves alive, and buried themselves."

But Paine's ignorance of human nature is nowhere so apparent as when he questions the authenticity of the

Gospel story on the ground that the four writers, in describing the same scenes, produce totally different effects. Had he been a biographer he would have known that contradictory evidence is not necessarily false evidence. Two men, reporting an identical episode, will invariably disagree over details and will often give an entirely different impression of its actors; the reason being that truth is determined by temperament, and people will see what they are looking for and hear what they are listening for, stressing what appeals to them and dismissing what does not interest them. The surest proof of the honesty of the Gospel-writers lies in the fact that as witnesses they so often disagreed, from which it is clear that there was no collusion. Paine, however, not being a biographer, believed that there was such a thing as absolute truth (meaning, of course, the truth he was capable of apprehending) and felt that he had finally disposed of the Gospels by saying: "It was upon the vote of such as Athanasius that the Testament was decreed to be the word of God; and nothing can present to us a more strange idea than that of decreeing the word of God by vote."

Paine, like many others, found it difficult not to confuse Christ with Christianity. "The most detestable wickedness, the most horrid cruelties, and the greatest miseries, that have afflicted the human race, have had their origin in this thing called revelation, or revealed religion," he said. "Speaking for myself . . . I totally disbelieve that the Almighty ever did communicate any thing to man, by any mode of speech, in any language, or by any kind of vision, or appearance, or by any means which our senses are capable of receiving, otherwise than the universal display of himself in the works of the creation, and by that repugnance we feel in ourselves to bad actions, and disposition to good ones."

Having set down the truth as he perceived it, he left "the reader to judge for himself, as I have judged for myself . . . certain as I am that when opinions are free, either in matters of government or religion, truth will finally and powerfully prevail."

## Chapter XIV

---

## GEORGE WASHINGTON

---

His ten months' imprisonment had soured Paine's disposition. It had taught him to hate, especially to hate the one person in whom he had reposed the greatest trust. George Washington had remained mysteriously aloof at a time when he should have moved heaven and earth to liberate the man who had done so much to liberate America; and all Paine's anger with himself for having put his faith in mankind came boiling to the surface and overflowed in scalding phrases on the head of the American President. His letters to old friends, such as James Madison, were full of "an indelible rancor" against Washington.

We must go back a little in order to appreciate Paine's feelings. He and Washington had provided the powder and shot of the American War of Independence. Washington could not have struck effectively without the force of Paine behind him. The one aroused the necessary enthusiasm, to say nothing of the necessary cash, which the other directed. But their early relationship was far more personal than that; there were even occasions when Paine acted as Washington's "publicity man." After the retreat across the Delaware he wrote: "The names of Washington and Fabius will run parallel to eternity." And when, early in 1778, a number of men (John Adams, second President of the United States, among them) tried to remove Washington from the command of the army on the ground that he lacked initiative, Paine came to the rescue with a *Crisis*. Believing that the war would be lost if the army and the country were distracted by controversy and that everything depended on national solidarity, he reminded the people of Washington's victory at Princeton, which was "attended with such a scene of circumstances and superiority of generalship, as will ever give it a place in the first rank in the history of great actions." He said that "the unabated fortitude of a Washington" had saved them again and again, and he appealed to the nation to emulate such an example at a time when men were "losing their all with cheerfulness, and collecting fire and fortitude from the flames of their own estates." Yet he was well aware of Washington's deficiencies as a commander and supported him partly because military rivalries and jealousies would have been fatal to the cause and partly because he admired Washington's character.

Many men have tried to describe that character, but it remains something of an enigma. It is difficult to resist the conviction that his friendliness of manner masked a frigidity of heart. People liked him at once. There were so many things in his favor: an attractive personal appearance, considerable charm of manner, an ability to put people instantly at their ease, an apparent interest in the welfare of others, a freedom of speech that was never malicious, a joviality of demeanor and disposition, a keen appreciation of sport, an enjoyment of good living, a relish of innocent fun, and not a sign of intellectual superiority. No wonder he made countless friends. How, then, did he come to lose so many? The answer seems to be that his popularity was contrived for a purpose; that, aware of his mental deficiencies, he relied on personal charm to achieve his end, and, that done, "scorned the base degrees by which he did ascend." But the answer may be a more subtle one. It may be that, finding himself in a position he had never envisaged and to which his abilities were not equal, he weakly sacrificed his human qualities in the cause of statecraft, becoming a slave to an office he had not the character to control. In either case he must suffer in our estimate of him as a man, however we may exalt him as a ruler. Indeed, the very qualities for which he was praised, and which were at first admired by Paine, should have warned his "friends" what to expect in certain eventualities. He was prudent and he was far-seeing; so prudent that he failed in gratitude and generosity, so far-seeing that he failed to notice anything between himself and the horizon.

To understand the sudden change in Paine's attitude towards Washington, we must remember that he had supported the General through thick and thin during many arduous years, then he had defeated the conspiracy of 1778, and that he was bound to Washington by the ties of fellowship in a common cause, admiration, and gratitude for help given at a trying moment; all of which, in a nature so simple and trusting as Paine's, created a feeling of warm personal loyalty and affection. To understand the gradual change in Washington's attitude towards Paine, we may recall that Morris had accused Paine of plotting with Genêt to stir up trouble in America, of drunkenness, of insolence to the minister himself, of opposition to Washington's pro-British policy, and of interference in matters that were no concern of his. Morris had also inferred that Paine as a French citizen was subject to the laws of that country, against which he had offended, and that an attempt to liberate him might result in his execution.

But what really influenced Washington more than all these things put together was his desire to conclude a treaty with England whereby, in return for her abandonment of six military stations in the United States, she should receive commercial concessions. This treaty, which was negotiated by John Jay, was not very credit-

able to Washington, who had been lulling French sus-
picions with the softest phrases of friendship while secretly coming to terms with England. Washington's
Anglophilia is explicable on temperamental and patriotic
grounds. His outlook and habits were far more those of
the English squire who made the English Revolution
than of the French lawyer who made the French Revolution; and he believed that the future well-being of
America was dependent upon a commercial agreement
with England. Thus for several years he had never lost
an opportunity of soothing British susceptibilities. He
had even sent an ambassador to a lady in Lichfield, Miss
Anna Seward, to explain how she had wronged him in
one of her poems and to prove his innocence of her
charge. The one thing, therefore, that he dared not do,
while John Jay was gathering the fruits of his diplomacy, was to ruffle the British Government, and nothing
at that moment could have ruffled it so effectively as a
public gesture from him on behalf of Paine, the Guy
Fawkes, the national villain, of the hour.

So, with the report of Morris to cover his conscience,
he sacrificed Paine for an alliance with the country they
had spent their best years in fighting, knowing quite
well that Paine would be his most dangerous critic when
the treaty was published; for at Paine's instigation
France had helped America at a critical moment in her
war against England. It may have been a sense of shame
that prevented Washington from sending a word of con-

solation to Paine, even from inquiring after him when Monroe reported his condition. But this is doubtful. Washington had ceased to be a man and had become a statesman; and Paine, had he but known it, was feeling sore at the neglect, not of the comrade he had once loved and honored, but of the institution into which Washington had first melted and then hardened.

On February 22, 1795, Paine determined, after much anxious thought, to write for an explanation to Washington:

"As it is always painful to reproach those one would wish to respect, it is not without some difficulty that I have taken the resolution to write to you. The danger to which I have been exposed cannot have been unknown to you, and the guarded silence you have observed upon that circumstance, is what I ought not to have expected from you, either as a friend or as a President of the United States.

"You knew enough of my character to be assured that I could not have deserved imprisonment in France, and, without knowing anything more than this, you had sufficient ground to have taken some interest for my safety. Every motive arising from recollection ought to have suggested to you the consistency of such a measure. But I cannot find that you have so much as directed any enquiry to be made whether I was in prison or at liberty, dead or alive; what the cause of that imprisonment was, or whether there was any service or assistance you could render. Is this what I ought to have expected from America after the part I had acted towards her? Or will it redound to her honour or to yours that I tell the story?

"I do not hesitate to say that you have not served America with more disinterestedness, or greater zeal, or more fidelity, than myself, and I know not if with better effect. After the revolution of America was established, you rested at home to partake its advantages, and I ventured into new scenes of difficulty to extend the principles which that revolution had produced. In the progress of events you beheld yourself a president in America and me a prisoner in France: you folded your arms, forgot your friend, and became silent.

"As everything I have been doing in Europe was connected with my wishes for the prosperity of America, I ought to be the more surprised at this conduct on the part of her government. It leaves me but one mode of explanation, which is, that everything is not as it ought to be amongst you, and that the presence of a man who might disapprove, and who had credit enough with the country to be heard and believed, was not wished for. This was the operating motive of the despotic faction that imprisoned me in France (though the pretence was, that I was a foreigner); and those that have been silent towards me in America, appear to me to have acted from the same motive. It is impossible for me to discover any other."

Paine showed this letter to Monroe, who persuaded him not to send it, hoping perhaps that Washington might yet write and clear matters up. The letter was put on one side and Paine waited patiently. But the months went by and no word came. His existence was being ignored by the Government of the country for which he had done so much and by its chief citizen of whom he had thought so highly. He felt humiliated, for such treatment was beyond his understanding and seemed to reflect on his own judgment of men. The hours he spent brooding on his wrongs began to affect his health, and by the late summer of 1795 he was seriously ill. Under the impression that he could not live much longer, he again wrote to Washington on September 20th, hoping at least to get some sort of explanation and so to satisfy his curiosity before he died. This letter, which was duly dispatched, asked for copies of any official instructions concerning himself which the President may have sent to Morris or Monroe. Such evidence alone could satisfy him that Washington had not connived at his imprisonment. Robespierre's order, which contained the phrase "for the interests of America," could only have been issued on the assumption that the American Government consented to the accusation; and by his silence Washington had tacitly condemned Paine to death:

"I ought not to have suspected you of treachery," he concluded; "but whether I recover from the illness I now suffer, or not, I shall continue to think you treacherous, till you give me cause to think otherwise. I am sure you would have found yourself more at your ease had you acted by me as you ought; for whether your desertion of me was intended to gratify the English government, or to let me fall into destruction in France that you might exclaim the louder against the French Revolution; or whether you hoped by my extinction to meet with less opposition in mounting up the American government; either of these will involve you in reproach you will not easily shake off."

Paine waited ten months for a reply, but Washington ignored his appeal. A feeling of bitter animosity towards the President, engendered by a deep sense of having been wronged and slighted, now took possession of Paine, whose restoration to health was marked by an open "Letter to George Washington," dated July 30, 1796, which was published in England and America. In this he printed the two letters already quoted and charged Washington with meanness and ingratitude to France, but for whose aid "your cold and unmilitary conduct would in all probability have lost America. . . . You slept away your time in the field, till the finances of the country were completely exhausted, and you have but little share in the glory of the final event. It is time, sir, to speak the undisguised language of historical truth."

Explaining his personal grievance, Paine wrote: "It was the duty of the Executive department in America to have made (at least) some enquiries about me, as soon as it heard of my imprisonment. But if this had not been the case, that government owed it to me on every ground and principle of honour and gratitude. Mr. Washington owed it to me on every score of private acquaintance, I will not now say friendship; for it has some time been known by those who know him, that he has no friendships; that he is incapable of forming any; he can serve, or desert, a man, or a cause, with constitutional indifference; and it is this cold hermaphrodite faculty that imposed itself upon the world, and was credited for a while by enemies as by friends, for prudence, moderation and impartiality." Paine thrust this point home in another passage: "Errors or caprices of the temper can be pardoned and forgotten; but a cold deliberate crime of the heart, such as Mr. Washington is capable of acting, is not to be washed away." It would appear that Washington was the first, as he was probably the last, of those strong silent men of action who only exist in the popular fancy: "By the advantage of a good exterior he attracts respect, which his habitual silence tends to preserve." But as we have evidence that he was talkative enough among his officers, we must conclude from this observation that "his genius was rebuked" when confronted by Paine's.

The peroration was harsh: "And as to you, Sir, treacherous in private friendship (for so you have been to me, and that in the day of danger) and a hypocrite in public life, the world will be puzzled to decide whether you are an apostate or an impostor; whether you have abandoned good principles, or whether you ever had any."

This letter was violently attacked by William Cobbett, a remarkable but unbalanced person who has always been the hero of emotional democrats. Cobbett's opinion of Paine at that time was couched in the following terms: "How Tom gets a living, or what brothel he inhabits, I know not. Nor does it signify to anybody here or elsewhere. He has done all the mischief he can in the world, and whether his carcase is at last to be suffered to rot in the earth, or to be dried in the air, is of little consequence. Wherever or whenever he breathes his last, he will neither excite sorrow nor compassion. No friendly hand will close his eyes, not a moan will be uttered, not a tear will be shed. Like Judas he will be remembered by posterity. Men will learn to express all that is base, malignant, treacherous, unnatural, and blasphemous, by one single monosyllable."

This was the general view of Paine after the publication of *The Age of Reason*, and Washington probably subscribed to it after the publication of Paine's "letter" to him. It is unfortunate that he never defended himself against the charges contained in the "Letter," because the judgment of history on this point must go against him by default. After making every allowance for the lies of Morris, it is impossible to acquit the

President of callousness to Paine, who left among his papers a piece of advice to the sculptor chosen to execute the statue of Washington:

> Take from the mine the coldest, hardest stone,
> It needs no fashion: it is Washington.
> But if you chisel, let the stroke be rude,
> And on his heart engrave—Ingratitude.

## Chapter XV

### NAPOLEON BONAPARTE

For a year or more after the publication of *The Age of Reason,* Satan and Tom Paine were the two most talked-of characters in England; and yet, as St. Athanasius might have said, they were not two characters, but one character. The country considered the attack on the Bible by this dual personality as a national insult and rushed to the defense of Jehovah. Every sort of denomination contributed its quota of abuse, and Gilbert Wakefield, a man with Unitarian sympathies, wrote volume after volume of religious ejaculations. Paine acknowledged one of Wakefield's books: "You have raised an ant-hill about the roots of my sturdy oak, and it may amuse idlers to see your work. . . . When you have done as much service to the world by your writings, and suffered as much for them, as I have done, you will be better entitled to dictate." Curiously enough, Wakefield did suffer a little for his writings, for when the sellers of Paine's work were prosecuted he fought for freedom of opinion and was rewarded with two years' imprisonment.

But Paine's chief antagonist was the Bishop of Llandaff, who wrote an *Apology for the Bible*, which did more to popularize the opinions of Paine than anything except the book that contained them. Bishop Watson should have remembered Dean Swift's warning to the clergy: that if they started to reason with critics of the creed they would awaken scepticism. The Bishop, who attacked Gibbon as well as Paine, was a little too honest to do his job properly; he treated Paine as a serious opponent and even gave way on certain points. Already he had written against political and religious coercion, losing promotion thereby. Whereupon he had recanted; but it was too late; all the preferments were going elsewhere; so he determined to enjoy himself, became more liberal in his views than before, and preached a sermon before the Bishop of London, who shook his head in a way that suggested to Watson that he would remain at Llandaff. "What is this thing called Orthodoxy, which mars the fortunes of honest men?" he asked himself.

Not all of Paine's critics were so reasonable, and when it became known that he was writing an answer to the Bishop the Society for Promoting Christian Knowledge instituted proceedings against the publisher of *The Age of Reason*, Thomas Williams, for blasphemy. This was in June, 1797, by which time both parts of the book

had circulated widely. Erskine, who had defended
Paine over *The Rights of Man*, was now on the opposite
side and acted as prosecuting counsel. After reading several of the less orthodox passages in the work, he rested
his argument on the fact that many great and worthy
men had experienced no difficulty in swallowing the
Bible whole. It did not require the shocked expressions
of the judge to settle the special jury's verdict, which
had been "Guilty" before they entered the court at a
cost of two guineas and a good dinner apiece.

Paine was a man who could not stop his pen from
forming words whenever he felt indignant; the result,
on this occasion, was a "Letter to Erskine" in which he
declaimed against the special jury system (the jurymen
being nominated by the Crown) and ridiculed the notion
that a committee of tradesmen were capable of deciding upon such a case as his: "Talk to some London
merchants about scripture, and they will understand
you mean scrip, and tell you how much it is worth at
the Stock Exchange. Ask them about Theology, and
they will say they know no such gentleman upon
'Change." For that matter it was absurd to appeal to the
law to protect God's word, for if it really were God's
word it would be like a prosecution to prevent the sun
from falling out of heaven. He had been told by his
critics "of the great and laudable pains that many pious
and learned men have taken to explain the obscure, and
reconcile the contradictory, or, as they say, the seem-

ingly contradictory, passages of the Bible." But that one
fact spoke volumes: "What! does not the Creator of
the Universe, the Fountain of all Wisdom, the Origin
of all Science, the Author of all Knowledge, the God of
Order and of Harmony, know how to write? When we
contemplate the vast economy of the creation, when we
behold the unerring regularity of the visible solar system, the perfection with which all its several parts re-
volve, and by corresponding assemblage form a whole;
—when we launch our eye into the boundless ocean of
space, and see ourselves surrounded by innumerable
worlds, not one of which varies from its appointed place
—when we trace the power of a Creator, from a mite to
an elephant, from an atom to an universe, can we suppose that the mind which could conceive such a design,
and the power that executed it with incomparable perfection, cannot write without inconsistence; or that a
book so written can be the work of such a power? The
writings of Thomas Paine, even of Thomas Paine, need
no commentator to explain, compound, arrange, and re-
arrange their several parts, to render them intelligible
—he can relate a fact, or write an essay, without forget-
ting in one page what he has written in another; certainly then, did the God of all perfection condescend to
write or dictate a book, that book would be as perfect
as himself is perfect: the Bible is not so, and it is con-
fessedly not so, by the attempts to amend it."

Erskine must have read this letter with a whimsical

detachment, because his attack on Paine had restored him to the favor he had lost by defending Paine, and he was now comfortably on the road to the woolsack. The imprisonment of Williams marked the commencement of proceedings against anyone who sold, lent, read, or talked about *The Age of Reason*; several people were even arrested for displaying the portrait of the author; and although it was not possible to declare war on Satan in quite the same way as war had been declared on France over *The Rights of Man*, the government did its best in this campaign of shadows by instituting a spiritual reign of terror at home. As a direct consequence of suppressing freedom of thought, heresy steadily increased.

Meanwhile the first ethical and theistic society had just been established by Paine and several others in Paris. It was called the church of Theophilanthropy. The congregation sang theistic and humanitarian hymns; there was an altar for flowers; and the walls of the meeting-place were covered with appropriate texts. Paine gave the inaugural address in January, 1797. This seemingly improbable episode in the life of a man devoted to common sense is easily accounted for. He had seen the failure of all his attempts to build a political republic for the physical needs of humanity; he perceived at last that men were not fit for one; and, because he could not exist without ideals, he fell back on the last resource of a disillusioned man, trying to create a moral republic for the spiritual needs of humanity. This seems to be the normal course of the idealist; when he finds that he has been duped by politicians, he meanders in the fog of utopianism; when he finds that he has been doped by priests, he wanders in the haze of theism or mysticism. Few men can face the mystery of the universe with the courage of Shakespeare:

> Men must endure
> Their going hence, even as their coming hither:
> Ripeness is all:

and leave it at that.

Paine, however, never in his heart believed that true religion could be organized. It was a one-man business. And in the same year that saw the foundation of Theophilanthropy he replied to a suggestion by Camille Jordan, a royalist, that priests should be restored to their churches, that public worship should be recognized by the State and that church bells should again be rung. "It is a want of feeling to talk of priests and bells whilst so many infants are perishing in the hospitals, and aged and infirm poor in the streets," wrote Paine. "The abundance that France produces is sufficient for every want, if rightly applied; but priests and bells, like articles of luxury, ought to be the least articles of consideration. No man ought to make a living by religion. It is dishonest to do so. Religion is not an act that can be performed by proxy. One person cannot act religion for another. Every person must perform it for himself."

In the past the priesthood had "fattened on the labour of the people, and consumed the sustenance that ought to be applied to the widows and the poor."

Religion was not the only subject that kept his pen busy during the years that followed his imprisonment. He wrote a pamphlet on "Agrarian Justice" which contained a suggestion that has since blossomed out into what are now called "death duties." He was among the first to realize that finance played a much more important part in the world than politics, and one of his intimate friends informs us that whenever he picked up a newspaper "his first glance was for the funds, which, in spite of jobbing and the tricks of government, he always looked on as the sure thermometer of public affairs." It is not, then, surprising to learn that in a pamphlet entitled "The Decline and Fall of the English System of Finance" he was able to predict the suspension of the Bank of England which followed a year later. This pamphlet had a large sale, the proceeds of which went to the relief of prisoners for debt in Newgate Jail, London. The English Government acknowledged this gift by confiscating the £1,000 due to Paine on the sales of *The Age of Reason*. William Cobbett was more generous. After reading the pamphlet he took back everything he had ever said against Paine and thenceforward reverenced him as a sage or a saint or something between the two or a combination of both.

All through 1795 and the early part of 1796 Paine

lived with the Monroes, who nursed him as if he had been one of their children. At last the abscess in his side dried up and his good health returned. A few people complained that he had "a great deal too much influence over Monroe," but when it was known that Washington had made a treaty with England there was so much anger against America in Paris that Monroe and his fellow-citizens were lucky to have so stanch a republican as Paine to help them through their difficulties. He was able to ease matters considerably not only for the minister, but for the English and American residents in France, and Monroe must have felt that all his kindness to Paine had been amply repaid.

In April, 1796, he left the Monroes for a holiday at Versailles, where he stayed with Sir Robert Smith, a banker, and his wife, whose letters had so much comforted Paine in prison. Here he spent the spring and summer, completing his convalescence among the woods and fields and in the restful society of his friends. His contentment for a while was complete, and, as usual when life was pleasant, he turned to poetry to express his release from care:

> Let others choose another plan,
> I mean no fault to find;
> The true theology of man
> Is happiness of mind.

Towards the close of 1796 James Monroe was recalled. His friendship with Paine, and the latter's renewed ascendancy in the diplomatic world, had grated on the gentlemanly sensibilities of Gouverneur Morris, who had repeated his old tactics by creating a prejudice against Monroe in the breast of Washington. Morris had actually reported Monroe as saying to several French friends that "he had no doubt but that, if they would do what was proper here, he and his friends would turn out Washington." It was easy to impose on the President, and Morris was a master of imposition; moreover, he was a royalist and a fellow-Anglophil, whereas Monroe was a Painite and a republican.

Having a family, Monroe put off his departure till the spring of 1797 and Paine made up his mind to accompany them. He went with them as far as Havre, where he experienced some uneasiness due to the presence of British frigates within sight of shore and to the feeling that Captain Clay of the Dublin Packet, by which they were sailing, was not to be trusted. Having already spent nearly a year in a French prison, he did not wish to spend the remainder of his life in an English one, so deferred his departure. His instinct proved to be right, for Captain Clay showed no desire to evade a British cruiser, the search party of which was rewarded with a letter from Paine to Vice-President Jefferson.

Returning to Paris, he stayed for a while as a guest with the family of Nicolas Bonneville, who had been one of the members of the small republican society founded by Paine in 1791. Bonneville, who was thirty-seven years old, had edited a number of papers in which the principles of Paine had been set forth, and had been imprisoned during the Terror. He was a poet and a publisher, spoke English well, translated parts of Shakespeare into French, issued the French version of *The Age of Reason*, and printed his own newspapers. He had been married for three years when Paine went to stay with him, and his second child was called after its godfather, Thomas Paine. He lived above his printing-office at No. 4 Rue du Théâtre-Français, and here, after a short visit as a guest, Paine became a boarder. As he gave away all the money he made by his writings on public affairs, he never had much to spend. During the eighteen months he remained with the Monroes he received something over £200 from the minister, but this was more than repaid by his services to the Legation. He probably paid his way with the Bonnevilles party by helping Nicolas to write his pamphlets and his paper *Bien Informé*, and partly with occasional sums from the small property in America.

One of his first visitors, after settling in, was General Bonaparte, fresh from his victorious campaign in Italy. The warrior was most effusive. He greeted Paine as the prophet of freedom. He rhapsodized, he went into ecstasies. "A statue of gold ought to be erected to you in every city in the universe!" he cried, and Paine inclined his head complacently as Bonneville translated the sentiment into English, while the crowd in the street outside vociferated *Vive Bonaparte!* "I always sleep with your book, *The Rights of Man,* beneath my pillow," continued the General. Paine was too polite to ask him whether the book was ever used for any other purpose than as a head-elevator. In time it became clear that Bonaparte had read not only *The Rights of Man* but *The Age of Reason,* for he made use of both works when feeling in a democratic or an iconoclastic mood. One of his most famous sayings came from a footnote to *The Age of Reason* which referred to the account of Joshua making the sun and moon stand still. Paine wrote: "The sublime and the ridiculous are often so nearly related that it is difficult to class them separately. One step above the sublime makes the ridiculous, and one step above the ridiculous makes the sublime again." With that sponge-like capacity for absorption which distinguished him, Bonaparte had read this with care, had let it soak in, and at the appropriate moment squeezed it out in the well-known epigram, *"Du sublime au ridicule il n'y a qu'un pas."*

Having said enough to convince any ordinary person that the war in Italy had been fought on *The Rights of Man* and that all his future wars would be fought on the same principles, Bonaparte asked Paine to dinner, begged for the honor of his correspondence and advice, and bade him farewell. Paine was impressed and pleased by the visit. He surrendered to the well-known charm

of the conquerer so far as to believe that Bonaparte
appreciated what he had written and done and would
be influenced by his advice. He was soon to be un-
deceived.

Bonaparte's presence in Paine's lodging was due to
one fact: Paine had been talking to members of the
Directory about an armed expedition to England with
the object of returning the royal family to Hanover,
of freeing the political prisoners, and of helping the
people to establish a democratic Constitution. Only so,
he felt, could the peace of Europe be attained. Bonaparte, whose aims were different, was all in favor of an
attack on England, and when he heard of Paine's
scheme he lost no time in making its author's acquaintance, following up his call by sending messengers at
regular intervals for Paine's advice on this, that, and
the other thing. At last he came to the point: he had
heard that Paine had a plan for the invasion of England. Yes, Paine replied, he had a plan. Could Paine
produce this plan? Paine not only could but would: an
expedition of a thousand gunboats, each carrying one
hundred men, full details attached. Would Paine accompany the expedition? Certainly Paine would, because one of his dreams was to see England free and
Europe at peace. Bonaparte was more concerned with
Paine's topographical knowledge than with his dreams,
but nothing could be gained by stressing the point.
Dreams, however, meant much to Paine and he had a

habit of backing them with hard cash: "Citizens Representatives," he wrote to the Council of Five Hundred, "Though it is not convenient to me, in the present situation of my affairs, to subscribe to the loan towards the descent upon England, my economy permits me to make a small patriotic donation. I send a hundred livres, and with it all the wishes of my heart for the success of the descent, and a voluntary offer of any service I can render to promote it. There will be no lasting peace for France, nor for the world, until the tyranny and corruption of the English government be abolished, and England, like Italy, become a sister republic. . . . The mass of the people are the friends of liberty: tyranny and taxation oppress them, but they deserve to be free. Accept, Citizens Representatives, the congratulations of an old colleague in the dangers we have passed, and on the happy prospect before us. Salut et respect."

Matters moved towards a final decision; the Military Council met for a serious consultation, and Paine was invited to be present. Almost every member of the Council was against the plan and Bonaparte fretted while they examined the charts and projects of their predecessors and weighed the pros and cons of the invasion. At last his impatience got the better of him. "Here is Citizen Paine," he declared: "He will tell you that the whole English nation, except the royal family and the Hanoverians who have been created peers of the realm and absorb the greatest part of the land property, are ardently burning for fraternization."

But it was beginning to dawn on Paine that Bonaparte was a little too eager. It probably struck him that the war would not be fought exclusively on *The Rights of Man,* and he may have pictured in his mind's eye "England's green and pleasant land" with its homesteads in flames, its crops destroyed, its inhabitants put to the sword, and all those other horrors he had already seen perpetrated in the name of Liberty. At any rate, his answer did not come up to Bonaparte's expectations. "It is now several years since I have been in England," he said, "and therefore I can only judge of it by what I knew when I was there. I think the people are very disaffected, but I am sorry to add that if the expedition should escape the fleet I think the army would be cut to pieces. The only way to kill England is to annihilate her commerce."

This opinion was backed by the entire Council, which much annoyed Bonaparte, who was still further put out by the suggestion that his unconquerable army, led by his invincible self, would be cut to pieces by a nation of shopkeepers.

"How long do you think it would take to annihilate the English commerce?" he demanded.

"Everything depends on a peace," was Paine's unaccommodating reply.

Bonaparte turned sharply from him and not long

after was on his way to Egypt. There is no evidence that he slept with *The Rights of Man* beneath his pillow during the campaign against the Mamelukes.

He never spoke to Paine again, but when he returned from Egypt he took the opportunity to be rude to the man who ought to have had a statue of gold, etc., etc. A dinner was given to the Generals of the Republic and Paine was a guest. Bonaparte passed by him, staring him in the face without recognition and saying aloud to General Lannes: "The English are all alike—they are all rascals." Paine, wisely, repressed a retort which, however effective after the affair at Acre, might have led to personal inconvenience.

The Egyptian business cured Paine of any belief he had ever had in Bonaparte, and we are informed by a caller at the house in the Rue du Théâtre-Français that "he entertains the most despicable opinion of Bonaparte's conduct, military as well as civil, and thinks him the completest charlatan that ever existed." He had good reason for thinking so, because when Bonaparte became First Consul, Bonneville was imprisoned for describing him as "a Cromwell." This practically meant the ruin of Bonneville, for after his release his newspaper was suppressed. Paine helped to keep a roof over their heads with the small sums he received from America. The next thing that happened was the Concordat made by Bonaparte and the Pope, which instantly resulted in the suppression of Theophilanthropy.

Yet, in spite of the fact that Bonaparte sent by Fouché a warning to Paine that he was being watched and would be transported to America on the first complaint, Paine put no guard on his tongue, speaking his mind freely and openly on every subject, from God to Bonaparte.

There is evidence in one of Walter Savage Landor's "Imaginary Conversations" that Paine unburdened himself without qualms to anyone who happened to call on him. Landor met him sometime near the turn of the century at the house of General Tate and described the meeting: "He treated me with distrust: I could not blame him. Many ran to see Bonaparte, many to see Mr. Fox. Paine, whose intellectual powers, compared with theirs, were as a myriad to a unit, was unvisited and avoided. Of his virtues I have only one proof: show me its equal." Landor also said that Paine was always called "Tom," not out of disrespect, but because he was a jolly good fellow. Many years later Landor introduced Paine into one of his Imaginary Conversations; but from internal evidence, coupled with our knowledge that he frequently drew on his memory to enrich his fancy, we may feel confident that the following conversation is no more "imagined" (using the term in the sense of "invented") than any biographical recollection:

"Wonderful it appears to me," said I, "that a nation

of late so enthusiastic for Liberty, should voluntarily bend to despotism."

"You have not lived among us," answered Paine. "The whole nation may be made as enthusiastic about a salad as about a constitution; about the colour of a cockade as about a consul or a king. This fellow has done advisedly in calling himself consul: it will hold for a couple of years: he will then change the name, and be tribune or emperor—tribune, if prudent, as the more popular, and as the people see emperors in the vilest of their enemies: urchins whipt and promising to be good, very good, for ever good, by Christ and Peter! but spitting at the flogger on being let loose, and holding out one fist at a distance, while the other draws up the waistband. Bonaparte wants conduct, foresight, knowledge, experience, and (the Council of Five-hundred knows it) courage. He will do harm, but not long. He lives in terror—What are you smiling at, Tate?"

"My mother had a proverb of her own," replied he, "that a frightened cat throws down most pewter."

"You will shortly see," resumed Paine, "the real strength and figure of Bonaparte. He is wilful, headstrong, proud, morose, presumptuous: he will be guided no longer: he has pulled the pad from his forehead, and will break his nose or bruise his cranium against every table, chair, and brick in the room, until at last he must be sent to the hospital."

"He has the finest army upon earth," said Tate, "and his enemies are down."

"If it were possible," Paine replied, "to be hurt by such enemies, he would point at them, nettle them, shout in their ears while they were sleepy, put crumbs in their beds, shorten their sheets, and empty foul water down their throats, till they contrived to break his shins for him by some machination or other. The army, with such means of recruiting it, with Glory for his crimp and Plutus for his paymaster, seems indestructible. If the earth can not do it, he will throw it into crucible after crucible; he will melt it in water or evaporate it in air. In other words, navies and climates can and will shake and dissolve it."

"Thomas," answered the General, "I never thought you a visionary; but now indeed I must think you one. I do not estimate very highly the man's abilities, and less highly still his prudence; but he is no fool; he will not throw away what he has."

"I will retract my words," said Paine, "at the first wise things he does. Smile, sir! it is rarely that the wisest man can do anything better, or anything on some occasions more difficult. Let gazetteers and hawkers be dazzled by the emblazoned names they wave about their ears, and hold out to us with fierce vociferations: but let calmer men ask themselves, whether they really think Bonaparte would have surmounted the difficulties and dangers that environed Three-fingered Jack? And

whether Three-fingered Jack would have thrown away
fifty thousand soldiers so inconsiderately and fruitlessly
as Bonaparte? There is not on record one who has committed so many faults and crimes with so little tempta-
tion to commit them. There is not a leveret three
months old that does not shape its course more saga-
ciously. Tyrants in general shed blood upon plan or
from passion: he seems to have shed it only because he
could not be quiet, and from no stronger motive or
better reason than he would have had for going to the
theatre or the chase. Depend upon it, this giddy and
insensate man, deserted of his armies and of his principles, will finish no better than he has been going on.
There are few who form their opinions of greatness
from the individual. His sword, his mantle, his strut, his
swagger, and even things which constitute no part of
him, are his greatness; such as his porters, his guards,
his soldiers, and the gilding on the ceilings of his rooms.
Not those who need the fewest, but those who have the
most about them, are the great; as though people, like
bars of iron, could be mended and magnified by adding
one to another. Even in quieter scenes than where such
excrescences spring up, if you see a gentleman go out
fox-hunting in his scarlet jacket and his velvet cap, on
a spirited horse, with merry dogs, and a couple of
grooms behind him, you consider him as a personage
far more worshipful, than if, ignorant of his condition,
you found him catching a rabbit in a hedge-bank with a

ferret. Ovid says, 'The girl is the least part of herself':
of himself as certainly the man is."

Landor further reported Paine as saying: "I needed
not have written that book (*The Age of Reason*): they
tell me the arguments are found in others: I had no
money to buy, nor time to read them. Gibbon was pensioned, I was prosecuted, for one and the same thing:
but he was a member of parliament, and wore powder."

"Eloquence is the varnish of falsehood; truth has
none. . . . That is eloquence which moves the reason
by working on the passions. Burke is eloquent; I am
not. If I write better than he does, it is because I have
seen things more distinctly, and have had the courage
to take them up, soft or hard, pretty or ugly, and to
turn them on their backs in despite of tooth or claw."

Finally Landor hinted that Paine was again finding
comfort in strong liquor:

"Good books, as you call them, make you comfortable: good brandy makes me so. I have the twelve
apostles in this bottle, and they never shall complain
that I hold them long imprisoned."

"At least, Mr. Paine, leave others their habitudes,
while they are harmless, and think it equally so to love
God as to love brandy."

"Ay, ay," said he, "jog on quietly, and let your
neighbor be robbed and plundered by any rogue who
may have the impudence to call him my son, or my
brother, or my sheep."

## Chapter XVI

## AT HOME

THE last two or three years of Paine's stay in Europe were passed in comparative obscurity. It is not easy to account for his continued absence from America. Every year he made plans for returning and every year he canceled them. He longed for home, and France under Bonaparte was no place for him. In so far as he was noticed at all he was extremely unpopular, because his published strictures on the Slave Trade aroused the commercial instincts of the French people, who called him *scélerat, bandit, coquin, assassin,* and all the other words used by that volatile race whenever they wished to express disapproval.

One of the reasons why he stayed on may have been his desire to help the Bonnevilles; another was possibly his dislike of John Adams, who succeeded Washington as President and who fully reciprocated Paine's dislike; a third was perhaps his renewed interest in mechanical matters. A close friend in Paris was Robert Fulton, who was then in the midst of his experiments in steam navigation, which in 1803 resulted in the appearance of a small steamboat on the Seine. Paine had been among the first to produce suggestions for adapting the steam-engine to navigation, and Fulton made use of all his ideas. Then, too, Paine was once more letting his mind run on a gunpowder motor, was busy inventing a crane, a machine for planing boards, and was manufacturing wheels for no specified object. Finally he had returned to his bridge.

Having heard that his main structural idea had been adopted with success for the bridge over the river Wear at Sunderland, for which, of course, he got nothing, he began to make improved models, writing to Jefferson in October, 1800: "I have now made two other models, one in pasteboard, five feet span and five inches of height from the cords. It is in the opinion of every person who has seen it one of the most beautiful objects the eye can behold. I then cast a model in Metal following the construction of that in pasteboard and of the same dimensions. The whole was executed in my own Chamber. It is far superior in strength, elegance, and readiness in execution to the model I made in America, and which you saw in Paris. I shall bring these Models with me when I come home, which will be as soon as I can pass the seas in safety from the piratical John Bulls." In connection with the second model, which he made by molding blocks of lead together, Madame Bonneville gives us a valuable glimpse of Paine in the domestic circle:

"This was most pleasant amusement for him. Though he fully relied on the strength of his new bridge, and would produce arguments enough in proof of its infallible strength, he often demonstrated the proof by blows of the sledge-hammer, not leaving any one in doubt on the subject. One night he took off the scaffold of his bridge and seeing that it stood firm under the repeated strokes of a hammer, he was so ravished that an enjoyment so great was not to be sufficiently felt if confined to his own bosom. He was not satisfied without admirers of his success. One night we had just gone to bed, and were surprised at hearing repeated strokes of the hammer. Paine went into Mr. Bonneville's room and besought him to go and see his bridge: 'Come and look,' said he, 'it bears all my blows and stands like a rock.' Mr. Bonneville arose, as well to please himself by seeing a happy man as to please him by looking at his bridge. Nothing would do, unless I saw the sight as well as Mr. Bonneville. After much exultation: 'Nothing in the world,' said he, 'is so fine as my bridge'; and seeing me standing by without uttering a word, he added *'except a woman!'* which happy compliment to the sex he seemed to think a full compensation for the trouble caused by this nocturnal visit to the bridge."

The family was often extremely hard up and Paine even considered the possibility of publishing a volume or two of poetical and anecdotal works. Since they would be "little better than amusing," he faced the prospect of making money by them with equanimity. But writing for anything except the cause of humanity was for him a fruitless labor, and nothing came of it. It may be doubted whether he would have been able to understand the desire of, let us say, a biographer to write a biography for the sake of its subject.

His days in the Bonneville home were filled with activity of all sorts. Most of his time was spent in his study, where he made his experiments and received callers. He always rose late, and to anyone who happened to pay him a morning visit his appearance was not prepossessing, for he would enter the study from the bedroom with breeches unbuttoned at the knees, without a coat, in a shirt that had perhaps once been clean, his hair unbrushed, his chin unshaven, his face unwashed. The moment he was up he glanced through the newspapers, from which, though he could not follow French when it was spoken, he was able to pick up all he wanted to know about finance and politics. That done, he discussed the day's news with Bonneville. Then, after making himself look respectable, he went out to call on friends, and always on foot. "I do not believe he ever hired a coach to go out on pleasure during the whole of his stay in Paris," said Madame Bonneville. In the afternoons he seldom failed to enjoy a sleep of two or three hours' duration. His most intimate friends, with one or other of whom he often passed an evening, were Joel Barlow, Robert Fulton, and Sir Robert and Lady Smith. Occasionally he went to an Irish coffee-house in Condé Street, where many of the Irish, English, and American residents used to meet and where he discussed the politics of those nations.

Except at meal-times he was usually at home and even when writing or experimenting he was always ready to receive visitors. "Not a day escaped without his receiving many visits," Madame Bonneville tells us. "Many travelers also called on him; and, often, having no other affair, talked to him only of his great reputation and their admiration of his works. He treated such visitors with civility, but with little ceremony, and, when their conversation was mere chit-chat, and he found they had nothing particular to say to him, he used to retire to his own pursuits, leaving them to entertain themselves with their own ideas." Such stray acquaintances carried away with them the impression of a man with a pleasant manner and a quaint way of saying unusual things; a kindly man, whose strong features and bright eyes made some of them feel uncomfortable and gave others a feeling of confidence.

Let us pay a call on him in the company of Henry Redhead Yorke, who had known him in England ten years before and who managed with difficulty to find

him in Paris a few months before his departure for
America. Yorke had also suffered in the cause of Liberty. Born in the West Indies in 1772, he had been a
member of the British Club in Paris during the Revolution, when the advantage of liberating England by
assassinating George III had been gravely discussed.
Not feeling that the murder of a king would be of
value to the state, he left France and was denounced
to the Convention as a faint-hearted republican. He
settled in Derby and joined a debating club, where in
a heated moment he announced that he had assisted at
the revolutions in America, Holland, and France, and
would "continue to cause revolutions all over the
world." This statement reached the ears of authority:
he was arrested, tried for conspiracy, sedition, and libel,
and sentenced to two years imprisonment in Dorchester
Castle, where he fell in love with the keeper's daughter
and married her. We do not know whether the effect of
his revolutionary sentiments on his domestic life turned
him into a royalist; but at least he had enough of his
early idealism left to seek out Paine when he visited
Paris.

Paine was not easy to find, because when Yorke inquired for him at a bookshop in the Palais Royale, the
bookseller, the bookseller's wife, the bookseller's son,
and a book-buyer who overheard the inquiry, began to
scream insults at the *coquin, bandit, scélerat, assassin,*
whose pernicious anti-slavery writings had caused the

Negroes to resist the French conquest of San Domingo.
Yorke tried elsewhere, and at length arrived at the
door of No. 4 Rue du Théâtre-Français. A jolly-look-
ing woman (Madame Bonneville) opened it. Did Mr.
Paine live there? After surveying him carefully from
head to foot, she admitted that Mr. Paine did live
there, but that she was not sure whether he was at
home. The moment Yorke entered the house she held
a candle close to his face and said:

"Do you wish to see Mr. Paine?"

"I am just come from England and am extremely
anxious to see him, as I am an old acquaintance whom
he has not seen these ten years."

That was enough for Madame Bonneville, who appeared delighted.

"He is taking a nap, but I'll go and wake him."

In two minutes she returned and showed Yorke into
another room.

"This," said she, "is Mr. Paine's room."

Yorke glanced round. He had never seen such a
filthy apartment in his life. The hearth was a litter.
Opposite the fireplace there was a board, which looked
more like a scullery-dresser than a sideboard, covered
with pamphlets and journals. Several huge bars of iron
stood in one corner of the room, two large trunks in
another. Three rows of shelves ran across a wall; they
were filled with pasteboard boxes, each labeled after
the manner of a Minister of Foreign Affairs—e.g.

*Correspondance Américaine, Britannique, Française; Notices Politiques; Le Citoyen Français,* etc. Yorke was shocked by the discomfort and dirt. How different, he reflected, was the humble dwelling of this Apostle of Freedom from those gorgeous mansions tenanted by the founders of the French Republic!

Paine shortly appeared, dressed in a long flannel gown. "Time seemed to have made dreadful ravages over his whole frame," Yorke noted, "and a settled melancholy was visible on his countenance." He asked Yorke to be seated and began to talk at once, though it was clear that he had completely forgotten who his visitor was. Yorke was a little mortified, decided that he would not make himself known at once, and referred to circumstances that had occurred while they were in company or living together. Several times Paine put his hand to his forehead and exclaimed: "Ah, I know that voice, but my recollection fails." At last Yorke mentioned an incident that recalled him to Paine's mind. "It is impossible to describe the sudden change which this effected," related Yorke; "his countenance brightened, he pressed me by the hand, and a silent tear stole down his cheek. Nor was I less affected than himself. For some time we sat without a word escaping from our lips."

"Thus are we met once more, Mr. Paine, after a long separation of ten years," said Yorke, "and after having been both of us severely weatherbeaten."

"Ay," replied Paine, "and who would have thought that we should meet in Paris?" After a few personal inquiries, Paine went on: "They have shed blood enough for liberty, and now they have it in perfection. This is not a country for an honest man to live in; they do not understand anything at all of the principles of free government, and the best way is to leave them to themselves. You see they have conquered all Europe, only to make it more miserable than it was before."

"I am surprised to hear you speak so despairingly of the future of mankind," said Yorke. "Surely much might yet be done for the Republic."

"Republic!" cried Paine; "do you call this a republic? Why, they are worse off than the slaves of Constantinople, for there they expect to be bashaws in heaven by submitting to be slaves below, but here they believe in neither heaven nor hell, and yet are slaves by choice. I know of no republic in the world except America, which is the only country for such men as you and I. It is my intention to get away from this place as soon as possible, and I hope to be off in the autumn; you are a young man and may see better times, but I have done with Europe, and its slavish politics."

Yorke was surprised to find Paine indifferent to the state of affairs in England: he seemed tired and pessimistic and did not even wish to discuss the influence of his own writings, saying, when Yorke confessed that he had altered his opinions upon some of the principles enunciated in *The Rights of Man*: "You certainly have the right to do so, but you cannot alter the nature of things; the French have alarmed all honest men; but still truth is truth. Though you may not think that my principles are practicable in England, without bringing on a great deal of misery and confusion, you are, I am sure, convinced of their justice."

Paine warmed up, however, when Yorke told him that *The Age of Reason* had lost him many former admirers. He indulged in the most violent invectives against the "villainous imposture" of the orthodox attitude, which he compared with his own sublime conception of the Supreme Architect of the Universe, and declared:

"The Bishop of Llandaff may roast me in Smithfield if he likes, but human torture cannot shake my conviction."

"The Bishop of Llandaff," replied Yorke, "is a man of too enlightened, tolerant, and humane a disposition to wish you roasted or any other man for differing with him in opinion. You cannot say that his 'Apology' does not breathe tolerance in every page."

"Ay, it is an Apology, indeed, for priestcraft," retorted Paine; "but parsons will meddle and make mischief—they always hurt their own cause and make things worse than they were before; if he had said nothing, the Church would have lost nothing; but I have another rod in pickle for *Mr. Bishop*."

Paine's friend, Jefferson, had recently become President of the United States, and there was a strong probability that he would offer some diplomatic post in Europe to Paine, who laughingly remarked: "It would be a curious circumstance if I should hereafter be sent as Secretary of Legation to the English court, which outlawed me. What a hubbub it would create at the king's levee to see Tom Paine presented by the American ambassador! All the bishops and women would faint away; the women would suppose I came to ravish them, and the bishops to ravish their tithes. I think it would be a good joke."

While he was staying in Paris, Yorke saw a lot of Paine, and one day invited him to dinner to meet a lady who was very anxious to make his acquaintance. Yorke warned Paine that the lady was a Roman Catholic and begged him to keep off religion. Paine promised to be discreet, and the rest must be told in Yorke's words:

"For above four hours he kept every one in astonishment and admiration of his memory, his keen observation of men and manners, his numberless anecdotes of the American Indians, of the American War, of Franklin, Washington, and even of His Majesty, of whom he told several curious facts of humor and benevolence. His remarks on genius and taste can never be forgotten by those present. Thus far everything went on as I could wish; the sparkling champagne gave a

zest to his conversation, and we were all delighted.
But alas! alas! an expression relating to his *Age of
Reason* having been mentioned by one of the company,
he broke out immediately. He began with Astronomy—
addressing himself to Mrs. V. (the Roman Catholic
lady)—he declared that the least inspection of the motion of the stars was a convincing proof that Moses was
a liar. Nothing could stop him. In vain I attempted to
change the subject, by employing every artifice in my
power, and even attacking with vehemence his political
principles. He returned to the charge with unabated
ardor. I called upon him for a song, though I never
heard him sing in my life. He struck up one of his own
composition; but the instant he had finished it he resumed his favorite topic. I felt extremely mortified, and
remarked that he had forgotten his promise, and that it
was not fair to wound so deeply the opinions of the
ladies. 'Oh!' said he, 'they'll come again. What a pity
it is that people should be so prejudiced!' To which I
retorted that their prejudices might be virtues. 'If so,'
he replied, 'the blossoms may be beautiful to the eye,
but the root is weak.' "

The moment Jefferson became President of the
United States Paine's nostalgia increased and his desire
to leave Europe became urgent. But he had to surmount
one difficulty and one danger. Knowing how freedom
of speech was rewarded by Bonaparte, he could not
leave the Bonnevilles to certain poverty; and, having

had sufficient evidence of English "justice," he did not
wish to be captured at sea. He mentioned the danger in
a letter to Jefferson, remarking that a ship from America to Havre had recently been ordered into an English
port on the pretense that a Swedish minister was on
board. "If I had happened to have been there, I suppose they would have made no ceremony in conducting
me on shore," he added. Jefferson promptly offered
him "a passage to this country in a public vessel," which
he refused because somehow the President's enemies
got wind of the offer and made capital out of it in the
newspapers. At last he determined to risk the journey
in a private ship, on which he would be the only pas-
senger. Begging the Bonnevilles to follow him to the
New World and promising to look after them as best he
could, he made arrangements for the journey in the
summer of 1802. The Bonnevilles agreed to join him
later if matters did not improve in France, and with
this assurance he prepared for departure with an easy
mind. Just before leaving, Robert Livingston, the
newly appointed American minister to France, gave
him a word of advice: "Make your will," said he, with
a smile; "and leave the mechanics, the iron bridge, the
wheels, etc., to America, and your religion to France."
It was a shrewd tip, and for the sake of his personal
comfort it was a pity that Paine did not take it. But
had he been able to think of his personal comfort he
would not have been Paine.

Rickman, his oldest and most loyal English friend, crossed the Channel to say good-by and to see him off. They journeyed together from Paris to Havre, and on September 1, 1802, Rickman stood alone on the shore, straining his eyes after the boat that carried the old republican back to the Republic of his dreams.

*Chapter XVII*

---

RETURN OF A CITIZEN

---

THE republic of his dreams! How did it compare with the Republic of reality? Fifteen years had gone by since Paine had left America, and in that period a society of men in a state of flux had stiffened into a social order. History was about its well-known business of repeating itself. With national security men had formed into parties and groups, hardened into classes and cliques; the "pale" had been erected, the "haves" within, the "have-nots" without; people were fighting not for freedom, but for place, not for country, but for dollars; commerce was backed by religion; to have social prestige was to be patriotic; to be rich was to be respected; man as a character, as an individual, had ceased to be admirable; if he did not represent something, some creed, some cause, some class, he was nothing. It was the old, old story. A number of individuals had fought for a cause, which had engulfed them. The cause had triumphed at the expense of those who had fought for it and was now in the hands of committees; the human being was enslaved by the institution he had created.

It is an unfortunate but undeniable fact that as men become more civilized (as it is called) they tend more and more to develop an institutional frame of mind. In time the state, or the religion, or the class, or whatever the institution is, becomes more important than the man; discord between nations or sects or classes follows; and at last human beings are sacrificed in a war that is not even remotely concerned with their personal interests. Paine himself realized the danger and had taken care to point out that the activities of governments should be severely restricted. He knew better than anybody that the moment men formed associations or societies or governments or committees they lost whatever natural virtue they possessed; that the lowest common mental and moral denominator prevailed; that when men arranged themselves into groups for mutual welfare they became more timid, less generous, less candid with others, less honest with themselves, more willing to take the easier way, more inclined to side with the strong and bully the weak, than when they acted as individuals. Also he knew that corporation was merely another term for corruption, that a man who would not pick his neighbor's pocket would cheerfully plunder society. But owing to some quaint streak of indomitable idealism in his nature,

Paine had not allowed his knowledge of men to lower his belief in them; he had always hoped for the best; he still imagined that in America, the country which owed its independence to his pen, he would be permitted to live in honor and to die in peace; with the result that his final and most terrible disillusionment, though it did not break his spirit, shattered his pride (the symbol of his belief in mankind) and shortened his life.

He was handicapped from the start. A generation which knew not Paine had grown up in his absence, and there were two things about him that the powers in possession had every intention of making known. His anti-slavery views and his attacks on orthodox Christianity were equally repugnant to the commercial classes, because they made money out of Negroes, and, not being yet secure enough to withstand criticism, they required the buttress of religion to support their designs. During the Presidency of Washington and John Adams the Federalist Party (which included the royalists and tories and self-interested merchants Paine used to attack during the war) had been the chief political influence in the States, and though the republicans under Jefferson were now in power, the leaders of commerce and society belonged to the Federalist Party; that is to say, the Federalist Party was run by the leaders of commerce and society. The arrival of Paine was a godsend to them, because by advertising his heresy they could blacken the character of his friend Jefferson. The game started at once.

After a very stormy passage, fitting prelude to his reception in the United States, Paine landed at Baltimore on October 30th. He announced the arrival of himself, his models, his wheels, etc., in a letter to Jefferson, following the letter in a few days to Washington City, where he put up at Lovell's Hotel. His arrival was heralded and received by the papers with abuse and praise, according to the color of their political coats. The defamers got more fun out of it than the eulogists, because they were able to describe him as a "lying, drunken, brutal infidel, who rejoices in the opportunity of basking and wallowing in the confusion, bloodshed, rapine, and murder in which his soul delights." Those were halcyon days for the journalist, who, when feeling a bit below par, could write "the loathsome Thomas Paine, a drunken atheist," or "Let Jefferson and his blasphemous crony dangle from the same gallows," without feeling that he was going outside the editorial policy of his paper. Jefferson received his "blasphemous crony" with warmth, had him to dinner at the White House, and shocked their political opponents by walking arm in arm with him through the streets on fine afternoons.

Paine could no doubt have had a post in the government, but he saw how things were going and made matters easy for Jefferson by publishing a "Letter to

Bust of Thomas Paine by John Wesley Jarvis in the possession of the
New York Historical Society

the Citizens of the United States," in which he declared that he would not accept an official appointment: "My proper sphere of action is on the common floor of citizenship." He noted the effect of his return on the Federal faction: "My arrival has struck it as with an hydrophobia, it is like the sight of water to canine madness." He wanted to know why the Federalists called themselves so: "I ought to stand first on the list of Federalists, for the proposition for establishing a general government over the Union came originally from me in 1783." But he was aware that a word lost all its significance when it became a shibboleth of a political party. Realizing that the younger generation knew very little about him, he addressed a series of letters to his fellow-citizens on the events of the hour, taking occasion to refer to his past experiences whenever possible. He also gave Jefferson a lot of advice concerning the Louisiana Purchase, which was the leading feature of that statesman's administration.

Over a million square miles of land west of the Mississippi had once belonged to France, falling into the hands of England and Spain when France lost Canada. In 1800 it again passed into the possession of France; but Bonaparte wanted money for his war against England and knew that by selling Louisiana he could at the same time buy the neutrality of the United States. He therefore sold it to the American Government for fifteen million dollars. This purchase by Jefferson de-

termined the future history of the States, because by
obtaining complete control of the Mississippi it opened
out the continent westward, with the result we know.

While Jefferson was contemplating an offer to
France, Paine wrote him a letter advising it, and gave
him a good deal of assistance before the agreement was
drafted. "I have half a disposition to visit the Western
World next spring and go on to New Orleans," wrote
Paine. "They are a new people and unacquainted with
the principles of representative government, and I
think I could do some good among them." He warned
Jefferson: "Everything done as an expedient grows
worse every day, for in proportion as the mind grows
up to the full standard of sight it disclaims the expedient. America had nearly been ruined by expedients
in the first stages of the Revolution, and perhaps would
have been so had not *Common Sense* broken the charm
and the Declaration of Independence sent it into banishment." A serious problem in this vast new province
would be the shortage of labor: "Were I twenty years
younger, and my name and reputation as well known
in European countries as it is now, I would contract
for a quantity of land in Louisiana and go to Europe
and bring over settlers." He was terrified at the prospect
of a large increase in Negro slaves: "It is chiefly the
people of Liverpool that employ themselves in the
slave trade and they bring cargoes of those unfortunate
Negroes to take back in return the hard money and the

produce of the country. Had I the command of the elements I would blast Liverpool with fire and brimstone. It is the Sodom and Gomorrah of brutality."

While the iniquity of slavery was occupying his thoughts, the evil of his heresy was exercising the thoughts of others, and one December day he received a letter from his old comrade, Samuel Adams, cousin of the recent President, John Adams. Having resigned the governorship of Massachusetts in 1797, Samuel Adams was now eighty years old. From the agitation over the Stamp Act in 1764 down to the Declaration of Independence in 1776 he had been the leading revolutionary figure in Massachusetts, and General Gage had been instructed to send him to London, where it was confidently supposed his head would adorn Temple Bar. When Paine came out with his appeal for American Independence in January, 1776, Adams was the first member of Congress to support him, and from that moment the two were fast friends. But Adams, who was known as "the American Cato," had inherited from his Puritan ancestors an unquestioning belief in the Bible, and when he heard that Paine was going to publish a sequel to *The Age of Reason* he wrote to protest: "I have frequently with pleasure reflected on your services to my native and your adopted country. Your *Common Sense* and your *Crisis* unquestionably awakened the public mind and led the people loudly to call for a Declaration of our national Independence. I therefore esteemed you as a warm friend to the liberty and lasting welfare of the human race." He then said all the usual things, to which Paine replied in a spirit of conciliation: "The key of heaven is not in the keeping of any sect, nor ought the road to it be obstructed by any. Our relation to each other in this World is as Men, and the Man who is a friend to Man and his rights, let his religious opinions be what they may, is a good citizen, to whom I can give, as I ought to do, and as every other ought, the right hand of fellowship, and to none with more hearty good will, my dear friend, than to you."

The persistent campaign of vilification at last had its effect on Jefferson, who by the end of the year was avoiding Paine. Not wishing to embarrass the President, Paine begged for the return of his models, as he was about to leave for Philadelphia and New York. His intention in bringing the models to Washington was, he wrote, "to have some conversation with you on those matters and others I have not informed you of. But you have not only shown no disposition towards it, but have, in some measure, by a sort of shyness, as if you stood in fear of federal observation, precluded it." Jefferson promptly showed that he was not afraid of the federalists by inviting Paine to stay with his family. The invitation was accepted, and after a few days at the White House, during which he managed to convince the godly females of the establishment that he was not exactly their conception of Satan, Paine left for his old home in Bordentown, his departure being signalized by a Federal Party dinner on Washington's birthday, at which this toast was given: "May they never know Pleasure who love Paine."

His journey northwards passed without incident, except at Baltimore, where Mr. Hargrove, a minister of the sect founded by Swedenborg, accosted him:

"You are Mr. Paine?"

"Yes."

"My name is Hargrove, sir. I am minister of the New Jerusalem Church here. We, sir, explain the Scripture in its true meaning. The key has been lost above four thousand years, and we have found it."

"Then it must have been very rusty," said Paine.

At Philadelphia he arranged for the reception of his bridge models at Peale's Museum, but no old friends came near him. One of them, Dr. Benjamin Rush, refused to meet him because his principles were "so offensive." Paine did not linger there, but pushed on to Bordentown, where he received an affectionate greeting from Colonel Kirkbride. Home at last, several weeks were passed in agreeable pursuits. He was well in health and happy in spirits; his head was "full of whims and schemes and mechanical inventions," and he was eager to build a workshop in which he could give shape to his ideas. Every day he walked several times from his home to the tavern, where he drank brandy and talked freely with those who showed a disposition to be friendly. It

was observed that he was usually too deep in thought
to notice anyone who passed him on the way, and that
he absent-mindedly crossed and recrossed the street
several times as he went to and fro. Owing to his religious opinions he was shunned by the more respectable
classes and even his one-time friend, Samuel Rogers,
Kirkbride's brother-in-law, refused to take his hand because "it had written *The Age of Reason*." Pictures of
the devil carrying off Tom Paine were exhibited in
public places; the clergy hurled anathemas at him from
their pulpits; loud imprecations were heard in the
streets whenever he came in sight; children were
snatched up by anxious mothers and carried howling to
safety; and doors were banged as he passed by the
houses of the pious.

Wishing to see James Monroe before he left for Europe to negotiate the purchase of Louisiana, Paine set
out for New York in March, 1803. Colonel Kirkbride
accompanied him the first part of the journey. They
drove to Trenton, the scene of the victory which followed the first *Crisis*, where they dined at Government
House. Their presence became known, a mob of the
godly gathered together, and they were hooted in the
streets. Kirkbride went to reserve a seat for his friend
on the New York stage-coach, the owner of which
cursed Paine as "a deist" and shouted, "I'll be damned
if he shall go in my stage." Kirkbride appealed to another coach-owner, but was repulsed with: "My stage

and horses were once struck by lightning, and I don't want them to suffer again." They were forced to proceed in their carriage, which was instantly surrounded by a crowd of Christians, who jeered at them, hissed, pelted them, execrated, and accompanied them down the street with a drum, playing "The Rogue's March." Paine, according to a local press reporter, "discovered not the least emotion of fear or anger, but calmly observed that such conduct had no tendency to hurt his feelings or injure his fame." Enraged by his tranquillity, the crowd turned their attention to the horse, which they managed to frighten by banging the drum within a few inches of its nose. Having in this manner sent the carriage careening down the road and vindicated the Christian faith, the crowd returned to their more material pursuits. Somehow Paine and his companion got safely to Brunswick, where the stage-master had been warned of their coming. How Paine reached New York is unknown; but from that time the hatred felt for him was extended to Kirkbride, whose health was affected and who died seven months later.

New York, being a large city, was not exclusively inhabited by Christians, and on March 18th a dinner was given him by seventy sympathizers at Lovett's Hotel, where he was staying. In certain other places, too, his health was drunk as "the Friend of Mankind," but his admirers and those who sought him out were mostly English, Scottish, and Irish immigrants of the laboring class, who were not considered proper company by the men and women who, fifteen years before, had been eager to entertain the "literary lion" of the hour at their homes. The doors of all the respectable houses were now closed to him. The Nicholsons, who had professed so much admiration and friendship for him, even Kitty Nicholson, whose marriage to Colonel Few, another of Paine's friends, had brought from him the tender and affectionate letter quoted in Chapter VI, in fact all the people who had been proud to claim his intimacy in 1787 and who were now the leaders of an exclusive social set, ignored him completely, comforting their consciences by accepting the fiction that he had gone to the devil in every sense of the word. He was a pot-house sponger; he allowed people to stand him drinks until he could no longer stand; he was quarrelsome and blasphemous; he never washed; his clothes were filthy; he was down and out and damned. Such was the tittle-tattle of the time, and it helped to solace his former friends for their neglect of him. The Fool in "King Lear" could have supplied him with the true reason for their behavior:

> That, sir, that serves for gain,
>   And follows but for form,
> Will pack when it begins to rain,
>   And leave thee in the storm.

There is, however, record of one evening passed in "respectable" company. Dr. Nicolas Romayne, the leading physician of the place, asked him to dinner to meet certain notable citizens, one of whom was John Pintard, founder of the Tammany Society, which had often toasted *The Rights of Man* and its author.

"I have read and re-read your *Age of Reason*," said Pintard, "and any doubts which I before entertained of the truth of revelation have been removed by your logic. Yes, sir, your very arguments against Christianity have convinced me of its truth."

"Well, then," Paine answered, "I may return to my couch tonight with the consolation that I have made at least one Christian."

He certainly made several Painites, because he was denounced with such venom from most of the pulpits in New York that he aroused the secret sympathy of many and the interest of all. One prominent Presbyterian could not control his curiosity and burst in upon Paine, who was sitting with some friends in a room.

"Gentlemen, is Mr. Paine in this room?"

"My name is Paine."

"Mr. Paine, and you gentlemen, will you please excuse my abrupt entry? I came out of mere curiosity to see the man whose writings have made so much noise in the world."

"I am very glad your curiosity is so easily satisfied."

"Good-morning, gentlemen." (Exit.)

The Presbyterian was "suspended" for his curiosity, and a certain Baptist elder was denounced for having sat at table with Paine, who naturally did not allay the passions he had aroused by public statements of this nature: "If, as the pious say, the misfortunes of infidels are evidence of divine wrath, then my hairbreadth escapes must be evidence of divine favor."

He left New York in June and went to stay with some friends at Stonington, Connecticut. While there Madame Bonneville and her three sons arrived in the States. Nicolas Bonneville had been unable to support the family and had sent them over to be supported by Paine, promising to follow, himself, as soon as he could. Paine at once placed his Bordentown house at the disposal of Madame Bonneville and arranged for the education of the children. In the autumn he went to his farm at New Rochelle, about twenty miles from New York City. Ten years earlier the house had been burnt down and he did not then think he would ever have enough money to build another; but the property was looked after by friends during his long absence, had increased in value, and was now worth about £6,000. He wished to erect a workshop for his experiments and to edit a "collected edition" of his works, but his schemes for a quiet life were wrecked by Madame Bonneville, who, tired of Bordentown, came to New York, hired rooms, and began to run up bills. Paine was annoyed. True, he had promised to look after the family's welfare should they follow him to the States, but he could hardly be expected to do more than to give

Madame Bonneville a house, enough to live on, and to educate her children. Anyhow, having no ready money, he decided to cut down a quantity of trees on his estate and with the proceeds to set her up in business. Meanwhile, not wishing to be saddled with any debts she might contract in the interval, he gave out that he was not responsible for her bills. He was promptly sued for her boarding expenses in New York, which he had refused to pay on application. Characteristically, having won the case, he paid the money, after which Madame Bonneville kept house for him at New Rochelle.

"It is a pleasant and healthy situation," he wrote to Jefferson, "commanding a prospect always green and peaceable, as New Rochelle produces a great deal of grass and hay. The farm contains three hundred acres, about one hundred of which is meadow land, one hundred grazing and village land, and the remainder woodland. It is an oblong about a mile and a half in length. I have sold off sixty-one acres and a half for four thousand and twenty dollars. With this money I shall improve the other part, and build an addition 34 feet by 32 to the present building."

Life was not wholly tranquil in this pretty retreat. First he had a slight paralytic seizure, a reminder of his old illness in prison, which, by affecting his hands, interfered with his work. Next the man who had farmed his land for many years, instead of paying his annual

rent, brought Paine a bill for fencing, which forced him
to sell more land. Becoming his own farmer, he then
engaged a man named Derrick to help him. Derrick
proved to be useless and was discharged. Possibly under
the impression that he was rendering a service to God,
Derrick in a drunken moment fired a gun one night
through the window at Paine. But the divine favor was
once more extended, and, though the glass of the window was shattered, the sill riddled with shot, and the
wall beyind fairly well peppered, Paine escaped injury.
Derrick was arrested, but Paine would not press the
charge and the case was dismissed. His reputation as an
infidel had of course followed him to New Rochelle
and the children of the neighborhood were incited to
steal his fruit. Paine raised no objection; indeed, to the
amazement of the young plunderers, he sometimes
came out and helped them to pick his apples, pointing
out which were the most edible. Like many people who
have had none of their own, Paine was devoted to children and never missed an opportunity of proving his
affection in the way they most appreciated—apples,
cakes, sweets, and cents were theirs without asking.

A year of country life was enough for Madame
Bonneville. She was thirty-one years younger than
Paine, who was too absorbed in his pursuits to make her
a congenial companion, and whose economical habits,
such as the use of newspapers for tablecloths, were not
much to her taste. She pined for the excitements of a

city; and the lack of visitors, due to his unpopularity, together with the embarrassment of living in a house where at any moment a gun might be fired through a window, made her restless. Paine sent her to New York, where she was soon earning a living as a teacher of French in various families. He was glad to get rid of her, and from the description of his household furniture in the following letter to a friend we may surmise that she was glad to leave:

"It is certainly best that Mrs. Bonneville go into some family as a teacher, for she has not the least talent of managing affairs for herself. . . . I am master of an empty house, or nearly so. I have six chairs and a table, a straw-bed, a feather-bed, and a bag of straw for Thomas, a tea kettle, an iron pot, an iron baking pan, a frying pan, a gridiron, cups, saucers, plates and dishes, knives and forks, two candlesticks and a pair of snuffers. I have a pair of fine oxen and an ox-cart, a good horse, a Chair, and a one-horse cart; a cow, and a sow and 9 pigs. When you come you must take such fare as you meet with, for I live upon tea, milk, fruit-pies, plain dumplins, and a piece of meat when I get it; but I live with that retirement and quiet that suit me. Mrs. Bonneville was an encumbrance upon me all the while she was here, for she would not do anything, not even make an apple dumplin for her own children. If you cannot make yourself up a straw bed, I can let you have blankets, and you will have no occasion to go over to the tavern to sleep."

The Bonneville boys stayed on at New Rochelle, where they were boarded at a school. Paine now began to spend his time partly at the farm and partly in New York. Having made himself responsible for the Bonneville family (Nicolas being prevented by the police from leaving Paris), he was burdened with financial worries and had to sell his Bordentown property to keep going. Bouts of illness succeeded one another and his temper was not improved by the persistent attacks made on him in press and pulpit and the ever-present danger of personal assault. His pen was still busy, for he wrote a defense of Jefferson, whose moral character had been impugned, an essay on the cause and prevention of yellow fever, and various contributions of a theistic nature to a journal called *The Prospect*.

In spite of a physical collapse brought on by eating too little, he suggested to Jefferson that he should be sent to England in order to help his friends there to frame a constitution in the event of a successful invasion by Bonaparte. But the President was not hopeful. Early in 1806 information reached Paine that one of his deistic disciples had been forbidden to hold a meeting in Philadelphia by the mayor of that city, John Inskeep, to whom he wrote: "I do not know who Mr. Inskeep is, for I do not remember the name of Inskeep at Philadelphia in 'the time that tried men's souls.' He must be some mushroom of modern growth that has started up on the soil which the generous services of Thomas Paine contributed to bless with freedom."

For some months of 1806 Paine stayed with John Wesley Jarvis, the artist, who painted a portrait and chiseled a bust of him. Ever since his breakdown from under-nourishment he had been in pain and was again seeking refuge from his troubles in brandy. One night Jarvis, who declares that Paine was easily put into a passion but easily appeased, left him alone after a long talk. Being awakened by a noise about an hour later, he descended to the sitting-room, found Paine drunk on the floor, and tried to raise him, but was asked to leave him where he was.

"I have the vertigo, the vertigo," said Paine.

"Yes," replied Jarvis, holding up the empty bottle, "you have it deep, deep."

"My corporeal functions have ceased and yet my mind is strong," continued Paine, still lying flat on the floor. "My body is inert, but my intellect is vigorous. Is not this proof of the immortality of the soul?"

"I am glad that you believe in the immortality of the soul and in a future state," said Jarvis.

"That is a wrong term," objected Paine. "We have strong testimony, I have strong hope of a future state, but I know nothing about it."

"As the soul will live hereafter, will it be conscious that it has lived now?" asked Jarvis.

"To live hereafter, and not be conscious that I have lived now, would not be identity; it would amount to nothing," answered Paine.

A short time after this episode he was prostrated by something worse than drink. "I was struck by a fit of apoplexy, that deprived me of all sense and motion," he informed a friend. "I had neither pulse nor breathing, and the people about me supposed me dead. I had felt exceedingly well that day, and had just taken a slice of bread and butter for supper, and was going to bed. The fit took me on the stairs, as suddenly as if I had been shot through the head; and I got so very much hurt by the fall, that I have not been able to get in and out of bed since that day, otherwise than being lifted out in a blanket, by two persons; yet all this while my mental faculties have remained as perfect as I ever enjoyed them. I consider the scene I have passed through as an experiment on dying, and I find death has no terrors for me. . . . As I am well enough to sit up some hours in the day, though not well enough to get up without help, I employ myself as I have always done, in endeavouring to bring man to the right use of the reason that God has given him, and to direct his mind immediately to his Creator, and not to fanciful secondary beings called mediators, as if God was super-annuated or ferocious."

Paine lost his temper with Jarvis, who would not let his servant read *The Age of Reason* because she could not reason. Paine refused to argue the point, greeting the excuses of Jarvis either with a "Pish!" or with a "Pshaw!" With the intention of helping him through his financial difficulties, Jarvis suggested that he should pretend to recant, write a book on the subject, publish it as a hoax, and make a large fortune. But he shook his head, saying, "Tom Paine never told a lie."

"Why did you not get married?" asked Jarvis once.

"Why, I thought that I had talents, and that if I married I should not be able to make a present of my words to the world, for its benefit."

Never having mentioned his early marriage to anyone in America, he was a little touchy on the subject, and when dining at the house of General Gates he became quite irritable over what appeared to be an innocent query.

"I always threatened, if ever I saw you, to ask you a question, Mr. Paine," began Mrs. Gates.

"Well, madam, what is it?"

"Why, I've heard a great deal about your being married in England. Were you ever married?"

"I never answer impertinent questions," snapped Paine.

His after-dinner snooze was still a regular feature of his day's program. One afternoon an old lady dressed in a scarlet cloak knocked at the door and inquired for him. Jarvis said that he was asleep.

"I am very sorry for that, as I want to see him very particularly," said the old lady.

Jarvis took her into Paine's room and woke him up. He hated being disturbed on these occasions and looked so fiercely at the lady in scarlet that she retreated a step or two.

"What do you want?" he demanded.

"Is your name Paine?"

"Yes."

"Well, then, I come from Almighty God, to tell you that if you do not repent of your sins and believe in our blessed Saviour, Jesus Christ, you will be damned, and ——"

"Poh, poh! it is not true. You were not sent with any such impertinent message. Jarvis, make her go away. Pshaw! God would not send such a foolish ugly old woman as you about with his messages. Go away—be off—and shut the door."

His visitor raised her hands in astonishment and left without a word.

In the year 1806 Paine suffered the most terrible blow that could be dealt a man of his outlook and temperament. Four or five tories, all of whom had lived within the British lines during the War of Independence, were the election-supervisors at New Rochelle, and when Paine came forward to register his vote it was refused by them on the ground that he was not an American citizen. "Our Minister at Paris, Gouverneur

Morris, would not reclaim you when you were imprisoned . . . and General Washington refused to do it," said the chief supervisor. Paine accused him of uttering falsehoods and said, "If you do me injustice I will prosecute you." The man got up and called a constable, saying, "I will commit you to prison." Paine looked him steadily in the face and he thought better of it. All the same, Paine's vote was rejected, and though he appealed to Jefferson, Madison, Barlow, and Vice-President Clinton, every one of whom sympathized with his plight but could apparently do nothing to establish his claim, he was disfranchised in the country which without him would still have been a colony.

# Chapter XVIII

## LAST TROUBLES

ALTHOUGH he was to suffer one more kick from his country, it was the supervisor at New Rochelle who delivered the knock-out blow. The idealism, which had sustained him through so many years of persistent toil and intermittent anguish, was henceforth dead within him, and with that loss went his hold on reality. Man sees life through the lenses of his own nature, and Paine's contact with reality was maintained by his idealism. He could only deal with humanity on a basis of benevolence. The inspiration and force of all his work, the motive of his being, was a belief in the freedom of man, a conviction that generosity and honesty would flower from that freedom; and as his sense of reality was rooted in such ideals, the discovery that what he had taken for honest earth was nothing but quicksand weakened his grip on actuality and made a mockery of existence. Because he could still believe in himself, his spirit held out gamely to the end; but as he could no longer respect the outside world, he no longer respected his body, which he allowed to degenerate.

No man has ever expressed his idealism in such forceful, simple, direct terms as did Tom Paine, whose failure to understand human beings can be gauged by his success in moving them at times of crisis. Under the spell of abstractions men will always act in a manner they would scorn in normal circumstances, and Paine's apprehension of reality was limited to seasons when the emotions of men were keyed up to a level where actions were fostered by ideals. Within those limits his grasp of essentials was firmer than that of any propagandist or pamphleteer in history. He spoke the language of the people for whom he wrote, spoke it so vigorously and clearly that action seemed to follow as a matter of course. Without the art of Rousseau, the wit of Voltaire, the rhetoric of Cobbett, or the humor of Sydney Smith, he could claim for his writings a more immediate and momentous influence than all theirs put together. He had not had the advantage, or disadvantage, of their education. He read very little, only knew one book at all well (the Bible), and what he wrote was quite spontaneous and entirely his own. For the effect of words upon action the first number of his *Crisis* has not been equaled, and the only work that has ever transformed the mind of a nation in a few weeks was his *Common Sense*. These were his best, his most vividly characteristic works, though they were forgotten in the tumult created by *The Rights of Man* and *The Age of Reason*. The fact that he wished to have "Author of *Common Sense*" engraved upon his tombstone showed his own preference; and after the bitter humiliation of his disfranchisement he tried to remind America of her debt to him.

The elation of his enemies at New Rochelle over his rebuff was expressed so loudly, and he was subjected to so much public insult, that he decided to leave his farm and settle in New York. His parents had lived to a great age and he had always felt he would do the same, but now he wished to die and believed the end was not far off. Worried about the future of the Bonneville family when he would no longer be there to look after them, he tried to sell his farm, and closed with an offer of ten thousand dollars, but the prospective purchaser died and at the widow's request he canceled the contract. Taking a wretched apartment at No. 63 Partition Street, New York, where he lived on bread and rum and very little else, he drew up a memorial to Congress asking for the payment of an old debt. He had never recovered the expenses of his trip to France with Colonel Laurens, when he had ruined himself by abandoning various literary projects and saved America by bringing back money and supplies for the troops. These expenses he now applied for and Congress referred his application to the Committee of Claims.

There followed a long period of suspense which told upon his nerves, and in great agitation of mind he wrote twice to complain of the delay: "After so many years of service my heart grows cold towards America," he said. When it was known that his claim had been unsuccessful, general satisfaction was exressed by the Christian sects. At last, it was felt, the Almighty was moving in the right direction.

This final kick was administered to a man already crushed beneath the weight of ingratitude. Although he was still occasionally to be seen on fine afternoons walking with Robert Fulton along the banks of the Hudson and watching the new steamboat that was about to revolutionize navigation, or strolling along Broadway deep in conversation with a friend, most of his time was spent in some miserable lodging-house, where he would drink more than was good for him, quarrel with his landlord, take snuff perpetually, live in a condition of uncleanliness and discomfort that was painful to his visitors, and rage against the iniquity of the world. He was utterly careless of his personal appearance and once went out in a friend's gig to pay a morning call dressed in a dirty old gown. When his attention was called to it he remarked, "Let those dress who need it." The complexion of his face had not improved with age. It had an inflamed appearance, and the nose, a prominent feature, had become carbuncular. He longed for death, passed hours in a state of helpless dejection, and was frequently discovered in tears. "I am very sorry that I ever returned to this country," he once lamented, and to such a condition was he reduced that France under Bonaparte seemed a paradise by comparison: "I know Bonaparte. I have lived under his government, and he allows as much freedom as I wish, or as anybody ought to have."

In 1807 "old Tom Paine," as he was known to everyone, made his will. Except for a bequest to his friend Rickman, his property was left to the Bonnevilles. He wished to be buried in the Quaker ground because, though he did not think well of any Christian sect, he thought better of the Quakers than of any other. "My father belonged to that profession, and I was partly brought up in it." If the Quakers would not permit it, he was to be buried on his farm. "I have lived an honest and useful life to mankind; my time has been spent in doing good; and I die in perfect composure and resignation to the will of my Creator God." With these words he bade the world farewell. At the same time he jotted down a few "private thoughts" concerning a future life. One of them sounded a less confident note than was heard in *The Age of Reason*: "I hold it to be presumption in man to make an article of faith as to what the Creator will do with us hereafter." Perhaps his diminishing hope of a future beyond the grave was due to a fear that he might have to mix with some of the people he had met on this side of the grave. But, if his aim was less steady, he stuck to his guns, and maintained that an after-life "is consistent with my idea of God's justice, and with the reason that God has given me, and I gratefully know that he has given me a large share of that divine gift."

When it got about that he had left practically everything to the Bonneville family, a man named William Carver, in whose house he had lodged and who had hoped to figure in his will, made an attempt to extort money from him by threatening, among other things, to publish a statement that he had had sexual relationship with Madame Bonneville, one of whose sons was alleged to be his. Paine treated the threat with the silent contempt it deserved. He was more concerned over the behavior of another man named Fraser, who wrote and published a "Recantation" of the heresies in *The Age of Reason*, ascribing the production to Paine himself. When called to account, Fraser pleaded poverty, saying he had failed as a fencing-master, a preacher, and a teacher, and had received eighty dollars for the work. This explanation was sufficient for Paine, who said: "I am glad you found the expedient a successful shift for your needy family; but write no more concerning Thomas Paine. I am satisfied with your acknowledgment—try something more worthy of a man."

In the summer of 1808 Paine was living in the house of a carman named Ryder, nor far from Madame Bonneville and her sons in Greenwich, then a village two miles from the city of New York. Here he got to know a Quaker preacher named Willett Hicks, whose cousin Elias was later to popularize so many of Paine's principles among his followers, the Hicksites. It was to Willett Hicks that Paine communicated his wish to be interred in the Quaker burial-ground. But his request was refused by that religious body. Deeply moved by this refusal, for he was in a weak state of health, he tried to conceal his feelings by saying to Madame Bonneville that the Quakers were "foolish" to adopt such an attitude.

"You will be buried on your own farm," said Madame Bonneville, to comfort him.

"I have no objection to that," he replied, "but the farm will be sold, and they will dig my bones up before they be half rotten."

Madame Bonneville assured him that the place wherein he was to be buried would never be sold, and he did not refer to the subject again. He was seriously concerned for the future of Madame Bonneville, recommended her to the protection of such friends as he had, and once, when she was obliged to draw money from the bank, he said, sadly, "You will have nothing left."

Through the latter part of 1808 his health slowly got worse and he could take very little exercise. Scarcely anyone came to see him except Madame Bonneville, to whom he complained: "I am here alone, for all these people are nothing to me, day after day, week after week, month after month, and you don't come to see me." He felt lonely for the first time in his life, deserted, and his mental anguish was intensified by physical pain. To the Ryders he was just "a cross, drunken, morose old man" who fouled his bedclothes and disliked being washed. Early in 1809 dropsy set in and at his urgent solicitation Madame Bonneville took a house,[1] which they shared. Paine was carried there in a chair towards the end of April and occupied the back part of the house, which stood by itself in a plot of ground. His regular physician was Dr. Romayne, who came to see him twice a week. Commencing at his feet, the swelling reached his body and he suffered continuously.

The moment it became known that the famous infidel was dying, a sort of pilgrimage of the sects began. Catholics, Presbyterians, Methodists, Quakers, tumbled over one another in their eagerness to get at him and extort a recantation. Two Presbyterians gained admission by describing themselves as personal friends, and before he could protest against their intrusion one of them managed to deliver an admonition:

"Mr. Paine, we visit you as friends and neighbors. You have now a full view of death; you cannot live long, and whosoever does not believe in Jesus Christ will assuredly be damned."

"Let me have none of your popish stuff," he cried;

---

[1] The site is now occupied by No. 59 Grove St., Greenwich Village.

"Get away with you! Good-morning, good-morning."
The reference to "popish stuff" is clarified by another
of his sayings: "The Bible has been received by Protes-
tants on the authority of the Church of Rome."

To another minister of God he was less polite: "If
I were able to, I would kick you out of the room." He
had a strong voice and this remark was made with sufficient conviction to secure the rapid retreat of the
minister.

Unfortunately, the only procurable nurse was stricken
with piety, and notified her religious acquaintances that
her patient was showing signs of contrition. Once she
heard him cry aloud in the torment of his spirit: "I
think I may say what *they* make Jesus Christ say: My
God, my God, why hast thou forsaken me?" And in his
bodily pain he sometimes ejaculated: "O Lord! O
Christ!" Such exclamations, when uttered, for instance,
by the victims of toothache, are not generally regarded
as indicative of theological unrest. But if Paine had
shouted "O Jumping Jehoshaphat!" it would have been
taken as a desire on his part to reopen the question of
biblical historicity; and the nurse translated his involun-
tary expressions of physical distress into the tortured
appeals of a repentant sinner. She therefore determined
to extract a confession in the presence of some one in
sympathy with her views. But Paine had given strict
orders that no one was to come near him without his
permission, for he was aware that his enemies would do

everything in their power to interpret in their own way whatever he might say in semi-delirium. This difficulty was overcome by the nurse, who, having primed a certain Dr. James Manley with all the relevant facts, sent for him urgently one night on the plea that Paine was sinking. It was midnight when Manley arrived. Paine was suffering acutely from his disease and calling on God and Christ to help him, partly no doubt because he was less familiar with the pagan deities. Following a few remarks of a prefatory nature, Dr. Manley addressed the sick man as follows:

"Mr. Paine, your opinions, by a large portion of the community, have been treated with deference . . . you have never indulged in the practice of profane swearing: you must be sensible that we are acquainted with your religious opinions as they are given to the world. What must we think of your present conduct? Why do you call upon Jesus Christ to help you? Do you believe that he can help you? Do you believe in the divinity of Jesus Christ? Come now, answer me honestly; I want an answer as from the lips of a dying man, for I verily believe that you will not live twenty-four hours."

The Doctor paused for some time after each question. Paine did not answer, but he ceased to exclaim. Manley continued:

"Mr. Paine, you have not answered my questions. Will you answer them? Allow me to ask again: Do you believe? Or let me qualify the question: Do you wish to believe that Jesus Christ is the Son of God?"

After a long pause, Paine, who had been lying on his back throughout this inquisition, unable to raise himself, lifted a hand, and with as much emphasis as he could command replied: "I have no wish to believe on that subject."

Having failed to achieve her object, the nurse fell back on the Bible, which she constantly read to him for hours at a time. He was too feeble to protest.

Sometimes an old friend turned up to say good-by, and one afternoon a memory of the past was tragically revived by the appearance of Mrs. Few, once Kitty Nicholson, who must have suffered a twinge of remorse when she heard that he was dying. Paine refused to take her hand. "You have neglected me, and I beg you will leave the room." She went out weeping bitterly.

Unable to retain his food, he daily became weaker, suffering all the time in every limb of his body. He could not bear to have the curtain of his window drawn, and though he seldom spoke during the last three weeks of life, he hated being alone, occasionally calling out: "Is nobody in the room?—Who's there?" When there was no response he braced himself and shouted until some one came. He was always afraid lest his room should be invaded by a religious enthusiast who, without witnesses, could swear that he had recanted.

Not long before his death, when he seemed to be unconscious, Dr. Romayne said to Mrs. Bonneville: "I don't think he can live till night." Paine immediately opened his eyes: " 'Tis you, Doctor. What news?" Romayne replied that a man they knew had gone to France on certain business. "He will do nothing there," was Paine's comment. Then:

"Your belly diminishes," said the Doctor.

"And yours augments," said Paine.

Following a night of tranquillity, he died, after a brief struggle for breath, at eight o'clock in the morning of June 8, 1809.

Madame Bonneville and her children, two Negroes and Willett Hicks accompanied the body to New Rochelle. On the way an Englishman asked Hicks whose funeral it was. When told, the Englishman declared that "Paine had done a great deal of mischief in the world, and that, if there was any purgatory, he certainly would have a good share of it before the devil would let him go."

"I would sooner take my chance with Paine than any man in New York, on that score," returned the Quaker.

A few sightseers had gathered for the ceremony, and as the earth was thrown on the coffin Madame Bonneville, placing a son at one end of the grave and herself at the other, addressed the spirit of her departed benefactor: "Oh, Mr. Paine! My son stands here as testimony of the gratitude of America, and I, for France!"

Ten years later William Cobbett, to atone for a past error of judgment and to arouse the social conscience of the English people, made a midnight descent upon the grave at New Rochelle, dug up the remains of the author of *Common Sense*, and carried them to Liverpool, intending to stage a spectacular funeral; but absent-mindedly forgot his mission. Since that time the bones of Tom Paine have disappeared; and now, like himself, they belong to no nation.

# INDEX

Lexington, battle of, 19
Llandaff, Bishop
antagonism toward Paine, 220
criticism of "Apology," 248
Lightfoot, Hannah, Paine's opinion of, 43
Livingston, Robert, advice, 251
Louisiana Purchase, Paine's advice re, 257, 258

## M

Marat, conflict with Paine, 146 et seq., 156, 168
Marriage, congratulatory letter to Kitty Nicholson, 93
views on, 9-11, 94
Marriages, 5, 8
Monroe, James, friendship with, 191-196, 226 et seq.
Morris, Gouverneur, enmity of, 125, 227
relationship with, 164 et seq., 174

## N

Nicholsons, association with, 93, 264

## P

Parentage, 1
Personal traits, see Character and personality
Philosophy, 15-17, 276 et seq.
(see also various writings)
Physical make-up, 80
Pintard, John, meeting with, 265
Pitt, attitude toward Paine, 127
Political activities
as exciseman, 7, 10 et seq.
Common Sense, 21 et seq., 29
(see also Crises, French Revolution, etc.)

Political philosophy, 254 et seq.
criticism of constitutional and parliamentary governments, 104 et seq.
natural and civil rights, 104
(see also various writings)
Political quips, 88 et seq., 107, 119, 135
Political views on religion, 125
Popularity and unpopularity, 74, 86, 108, 126, 130, 137, 150, 194, 196, 217, 219 et seq., 262 et seq.

## Q

Quakers, Paine's opinion of, 40, 42

## R

Release from prison, 191, 193
Religious background, 2
Religious views, see Views on religion
Return to America, 251, 253 et seq.
Revolutionary War, 19, 31 et seq., 44, 60
end, 67
financial difficulties, 61, 62
Deane affair, see Deane affair.
Rights of Man
effect, 149, 150
quotations, 102 et seq.
reception in America, 109
success in England, 108
trial, 128, 133
Rights of Man, Part II
dedication, 118
publication delayed, 116
effect on public, 135
quotations, 119
Robespierre, relations with, 162, 189